COVID-19, Business, and Economy in Malaysia

Part of a mini-series of Focus books on COVID-19 in Malaysia, the chapters in this book address the pandemic's impact on business and the economy in Malaysia.

Covering a range of challenges and opportunities for business and the economy over a year-long period, starting from Malaysia's first pandemic lockdown in March 2020 to the state of the country as of May 1, 2021, the contributors highlight the impact of the pandemic on the Malaysian business and economy and how Malaysians are finding ways to adapt and rise above adversity. They illustrate how the pandemic has affected businesses and anticipate the prospects for the Malaysian economy going forward. This is also an opportunity to witness how researchers from multiple disciplines can join forces during challenging times to deliver insightful research with impact. More importantly, there are many lessons to be learned from the successes and failures in responding to the pandemic in this developing Southeast Asian economy.

A fascinating read for individuals with an interest in crisis adaptation in non-Western contexts, especially those with a particular interest in Malaysia or Southeast Asia more generally.

Weng Marc Lim is the Chief Editor of the Business and Economy section of the *COVID-19 in Malaysia Multidisciplinary Series.* He is an Adjunct Professor of Swinburne Business School at Swinburne University of Technology's home campus in Australia and a Professor and the Head of the School of Business at Swinburne University of Technology's international branch campus in Malaysia. His research interests include business, consumer, and government (BCG) research. He has (co)developed the pro-active model for peer-reviewing in premier journals, the data partitioning technique for experimental research, the "how-to" guide for bibliometric analysis, the Scientific Procedures and Rationales for Systematic Literature Reviews (SPAR-4-SLR) protocol, the agency and reactance theory of crowding, the theory of behavioural control, the dialectic antidotes to critics of the technology acceptance model, and the integrated information systems-consumer behaviour (IS-CB) model for e-shopping.

Surinderpal Kaur is the Editor of the *COVID-19 in Malaysia Multidisciplinary Series.* She is an Associate Professor and the Dean of the Faculty of Languages and Linguistics, Universiti Malaya, Malaysia. She attained her PhD from Lancaster University, UK. Her research interests include media discourses and multimodality, focusing specifically on public discourses in mainstream and social media that relate to public health, migration, and terrorism issues. She has been actively involved with Universiti Malaya's social outreach initiatives to offer solutions to the mental health challenges faced by Malaysian during the COVID-19 pandemic (Caring Together/UMPrihatin), focusing specifically on the social media platforms of Telegram and Facebook. She is currently compiling a database of data and research from all over the world to help Malaysian scholars in their research on COVID-19.

Huey Fen Cheong is the co-editor and Managing Editor of the *COVID-19 in Malaysia Multidisciplinary Series.* She is a Senior Lecturer in the Department of English Language, Faculty of Languages and Linguistics, Universiti Malaya, Malaysia. Her research interests are interdisciplinary, from gender studies and linguistics to marketing and psychology. Her works are usually humanitarian, from gender equality (for men and women) and anti-racism (skin whitening and Black Lives Matter) to decolonisation of academia. The latter explains the initiative behind this book series in creating a platform for researchers to study the COVID-19 pandemic in Malaysia, which addresses the lack of COVID-19 research and publication in Southeast Asia. She is also the Founder of the Facebook group, (Post-)COVID job market in Malaysia (https://www.facebook.com/groups/2805574166392321), which shares information about the New Normal and the Next Normal of employment and employability during this challenging time.

COVID-19 in Asia Series

COVID-19, Business, and Economy in Malaysia
Retrospective and Prospective Perspectives
Edited by Weng Marc Lim, Surinderpal Kaur, and Huey Fen Cheong

COVID-19, Education, and Literacy in Malaysia
Social Contexts of Teaching and Learning
Edited by Ambigapathy Pandian, Surinderpal Kaur and Huey Fen Cheong

COVID-19 and Psychology in Malaysia
Psychosocial Effects, Coping, and Resilience
Edited by D. Gerard Joseph Louis, Surinderpal Kaur and Huey Fen Cheong

COVID-19, Business, and Economy in Malaysia

Retrospective and Prospective Perspectives

Edited by Weng Marc Lim, Surinderpal Kaur, and Huey Fen Cheong

LONDON AND NEW YORK

First published 2022
by Routledge
2 Park Square, Milton Park, Abingdon, Oxon OX14 4RN

and by Routledge
605 Third Avenue, New York, NY 10158

Routledge is an imprint of the Taylor & Francis Group, an Informa business

British Library Cataloguing-in-Publication Data
A catalogue record for this book is available from the British Library.

Library of Congress Cataloguing-in-Publication Data
A catalog record has been requested for this book.

ISBN: 978-1-032-02285-7 (hbk)
ISBN: 978-1-032-02288-8 (pbk)
ISBN: 978-1-003-18274-0 (ebk)

DOI: 10.4324/9781003182740

Typeset in Galliard
by KnowledgeWorks Global Ltd.

Contents

Tables

Figures

Contributors

*Arranged according to the alphabetical order of the last names.

Cecilia Yin Mei Cheong is a Senior Lecturer in the Department of English Language, Faculty of Languages and Linguistics, Universiti Malaya, Malaysia, for more than 25 years. Her research interests include critical genre analysis, multimodal discourse analysis, English for specific purposes, communication and professional discourse. She is a Principal Investigator of various research projects involving the study of professional genres, multimodal texts and discourses. Cecilia is an external reviewer for ISI-indexed, Scopus-indexed and peer-reviewed journals. Currently, she is the Assistant Secretary of the Malaysian Association of Applied Linguistics (MAAL), an affiliate of the Association Internationale de Linguistique (AILA).

Huey Fen Cheong is the author of Chapter 8 as well as the co-editor of the book. Please refer to the editor's biography in front.

Chorng Yuan Fung is a multidisciplinary academic and researcher. He is a Course Director and a Senior Lecturer at Swinburne University of Technology's Sarawak campus in Malaysia. He is an accountant by profession and holds a Master of Science in human resource development and a PhD in educational psychology. His research interests include human resource development, organisational behaviour and pedagogy in higher education. Fung also publishes regularly in these areas. Currently, Fung is a Member of the Business and Social Innovation Centre, the Research Cluster Leader for the Business Innovation Cluster and a Portfolio Leader in one of the research clusters in the Education Research Centre. He writes regularly in print media and serves as a corporate trainer on human resource development.

Fumitaka Furuoka is an Associate Professor at Asia-Europe Institute, Universiti Malaya, Malaysia. His research interests include labour economics and international economics.

Asanka Gunasekara is a Lecturer at Swinburne Business School, Swinburne University of Technology, Australia. Asanka's main research interests are in the areas of social and organisational inclusion of migrants. She is particularly interested in skilled migrants' acculturation, wellbeing and career success. She is also interested in employee and organisational mindfulness and wellbeing studies.

Nabila Huda Ibrahim is a Graduate Research Assistant at Malaysia-Korea Research Center, Universiti Malaya, Malaysia. Currently, she is pursuing PhD in the field of social and behavioural studies. She obtained her master's degree from Universiti Teknologi MARA, Shah Alam, Malaysia in administrative science. She has a strong interest in social science research in the field of cultural anthropology, sociology, social psychology, leadership, strategic management, policy analysis and socio-economic. She is also keen in doing research and innovation that speak to the needs of society. She has won the Diamond Award for her innovative product called the "Employee Creativity and Innovation Scorecard".

Siti Nurhayati Khairatun is a Senior Lecturer at the Department of Food Service and Management, Faculty of Food Science and Technology, Universiti Putra Malaysia, Malaysia. She holds two bachelor degrees: LLB (Hons) and BSc in culinary arts management. She graduated with a Master degree in gastronomy and a doctoral degree in hospitality management with a minor in food sciences. Before joining academia, she worked in the legal and food industry for more than 15 years. Her research interests include food and education, food business management, food regulatory and policy, food crime management and food tourism.

Su Teng Lee has both academic and industry experience. A seasoned human resource (HR) professional with years of progressive experience. Her broad experience includes hands-on involvement in managing the full spectrum of HR, working with HR information systems, spearheading HR business contingency plans and being a HR representative for acquisition exercise. She has now moved on to her academic career after her PhD with the Faculty of Business and Accountancy, Universiti Malaya, Malaysia, where she teaches HR. Her research is interdisciplinary and addresses issues of generational cohort, employee engagement, and HR more broadly.

Jingyi Li is a PhD candidate at the Asia-Europe Institute, Universiti Malaya, Malaysia. Her research interests include COVID-19 and tourism studies.

Beatrice Lim is a Senior Lecturer at the Faculty of Business, Economics and Accountancy, Universiti Malaysia Sabah, Malaysia. Her research interests include labour economics and gender studies.

Weng Marc Lim is the author of Chapter 1 as well as the Chief Editor of this book. Please refer to the editor's biography in front.

Firuza Begham Mustafa is an Associate Professor at the Department of Geography, Faculty of Arts and Social Sciences, Universiti Malaya, Malaysia. She is specialised in agriculture, geography, environment, aquaculture and geophysical fields. She has collaborated with local and international researchers and produced more than 100 publications, including WOS-ISI journals, books, book chapters, conferences papers and posters. She has written book chapters in international books published by Pearson Learning Solutions, Springer, Taylor & Francis, and Emerging Technologies and Research. She has several intellectual property rights (IPRs), and won many medals for research and publication.

Lin Dar Ong is a Senior Lecturer at the Faculty of Business and Accountancy, Universiti Malaya, Malaysia. She holds a Bachelor's degree with honours in business administration from Universiti Malaya and a Master's degree in business administration from Universiti Utara Malaysia. She completed her PhD at Universiti Malaya. Her research interests include management, organisational behaviour, leadership, business communication, and human resource management. She has authored more than three books and published in numerous journals indexed on the Web of Science.

Khairul Hanim Pazim is a Lecturer at the Faculty of Business, Economics and Accountancy, Universiti Malaysia Sabah, Malaysia. Her research interests include labour economics and ageing studies.

Noraida Saidi holds a Master degree in forensic accounting and financial criminology from Universiti Teknologi MARA, Malaysia. She is a Senior Lecturer at the Faculty of Accountancy, Universiti Teknologi MARA, Kelantan branch. Her research interests include financial accounting, financial reporting and forensic accounting.

Normaizatul Akma Saidi holds a PhD in finance from Universiti Putra Malaysia, Malaysia. She is a Senior Lecturer at the Faculty of Hospitality, Tourism and Wellness, Universiti Malaysia Kelantan, Malaysia. Her research interests include finance and financial risk.

Preface

Like the heart that keeps humans alive, the business facilitates exchange, and that is the reason economies exist worldwide; without business, the economies would cease to exist.

In 2020, the world, including Malaysia, experienced an unprecedented global humanitarian crisis—that is, the coronavirus disease 2019 (COVID-19) pandemic—which threatens the existence of business and therefore the economy. The massive lockdowns and restrictions imposed worldwide to control the pandemic were no doubt necessary, but the lessons learned will need to be unpacked and deliberated so that the world can be better prepared to combat such crises in the future.

This book entitled *COVID-19, Business, and Economy in Malaysia: Retrospective and Prospective Perspectives* is a seminal endeavor that seeks to provide insights into the impact of the COVID-19 pandemic on business and economy, with a particular focus on Malaysia. Unlike independent articles that may exist, this book has purposefully curated a collection of pertinent topics predicated on research that have considered a year-long of events in addition to undergoing a rigorous peer review process, and thus, readers can gain an encompassing perspective with high-quality insights into the business and economic aspects of COVID-19 in Malaysia. The peer reviews were both constructive and developmental, thereby contributing to capability building and continuous improvement among enthusiastic scholars—as authors and as peer reviewers—in and out of Malaysia.

Chapters 1 to 7 offer retrospective insights, whereas Chapters 8 and 9 provide prospective insights into business and economy in light of the COVID-19 pandemic in Malaysia. Multiple research designs have been relied upon, which include the use of primary and secondary data.

Chapter 1 by Weng Marc Lim from Swinburne University of Technology Australia and Malaysia introduces the concept of the quarantine economy and discusses the preventive and support measures implemented by the Government of Malaysia to combat the COVID-19 pandemic and cushion the shocks to the Malaysian economy. The macro insights from this chapter lay the foundational understanding for readers to appreciate the insights in the subsequent chapters of this book.

Chapter 2 by Firuza Begham Mustafa from Universiti Malaya explores the impact of the COVID-19 pandemic on the Malaysian agriculture industry, which has been noted in Chapter 1 as one of the biggest and most productive industries in the Malaysian economy. Though agriculture work has increased during the COVID-19 pandemic, this chapter exposes the issues pertaining to farmer income and food supply chain, which are both important to meet food demand and safeguard food security in the country, along with several pertinent recommendations to remedy the issues uncovered.

Chapter 3 by Noraida Saidi from Universiti Teknologi MARA and Normaizatul Akma Saidi from Universiti Malaysia Kelantan examines the impact of COVID-19 on business resilience through a survey of small and medium enterprise (SME) owners in Kelantan, a developing state in Malaysia. The authors reveal that SMEs in Malaysia initially found it difficult to manage and run their business when the COVID-19 pandemic first struck the Malaysian economy, but this difficulty was quickly alleviated as SMEs engaged in transformational leadership and took swift action to migrate their operations offline to online (e.g., digital marketing, social media). The SMEs were also found to engage in financial management practices such as working capital management, inventory management, debt management, cash flow management, bookkeeping, and cost saving analysis, which help them to navigate, remain resilient, and survive the COVID-19 pandemic.

Chapter 4 by Nabila Huda Ibrahim from Universiti Malaya investigates corporate social responsibility among business players in the Malaysian economy during the COVID-19 pandemic. The chapter provides evidence that corporate social responsibility activities, such as the provision of food supplies, personal protective equipment (e.g., face mask, hand sanitizer), sponsored products (e.g., Internet), training, and financial aid, were prominent among business players in the country despite the unprecedented challenges that their business encountered in combating the economic and public health crisis.

Chapter 5 by Lin Dar Ong and Su Teng Lee from Universiti Malaya sheds light on human capital practices among companies in Malaysia during the COVID-19 pandemic. The authors reveal the new normal in the labor market from the employer and employee perspectives, wherein the former is characterized by the rise in remote work, the prominence of health and safety precautions, the reconfigurations to maintain a high-performance work system, and the adherence to standard operating procedures by the government, whereas the latter involves the adjustment to remote and hybrid work arrangements, the adherence to COVID-19-related directives and rules at the workplace, and the management of physical and mental wellbeing. They also provide recommendations on how employers and employees can go about dealing with these challenges and expectations in the new normal.

Chapter 6 by Siti Nurhayati Khairatun from Universiti Putra Malaysia concentrates on the loan moratorium policy that was implemented by the Government of Malaysia to help business players to weather the challenges during the COVID-19 pandemic using the hospitality industry as a case. The chapter indicates that though the loan moratorium is a public policy that is welcomed, the impact of such a policy alone is of little help. Instead, consultation with industry players, a longer period for the loan moratorium, and packaging the policy alongside other assistance from the stimulus package in a hassle-free manner (e.g., integrated and relaxed application and terms and conditions) can be considered to alleviate anxiety and the challenges faced, as suggested by the restaurateurs who participated in the study.

Chapter 7 by Jingyi Li and Fumitaka Furuoka from Universiti Malaya and Beatrice Fui Yee Lim and Khairul Hanim Pazim from Universiti Malaysia Sabah investigate domestic travel inclination among Malaysians, thereby shedding light on the impact of the COVID-19 pandemic on the tourism industry in Malaysia. Using the theory of planned behavior, the authors reveal that attitude, subjective norms, and behavioral controls significantly influenced domestic travel intentions before and during the COVID-19 pandemic, with significant differences revealed between genders, wherein both males and females were less inclined to travel during the COVID-19 pandemic than before the pandemic.

Chapter 8 by Huey Fen Cheong and Cecilia Yin Mei Cheong from Universiti Malaya explores the job preparedness of future jobseekers post the COVID-19 pandemic in Malaysia. Using a sample of third-year undergraduates who attended a job preparation course at a Malaysian university prior to an internship and entering the labor market, the authors highlight that most future jobseekers are unaware of the exact changes that have transpired in the labor market as a result of the COVID-19 pandemic, though they do have a rough sense of the potential jobs that could avail in the evolving future of work, ranging from employed and entrepreneurial work to gig work. More importantly, the authors note that future jobseekers understand that though they are in no position to guarantee employment, they realize that they are responsible for their own employability, which involves upskilling and reskilling to meet the demands of jobs in the future.

Chapter 9 by Chorng Yuan Fung and Asanka Gunasekara from Swinburne University of Technology Malaysia and Australia builds on the insights from Chapters 5 and 8 and sheds additional light on the challenges that employees face during the COVID-19 pandemic and the ways in which contemporary career approaches can be curated to address the issues pertaining to career management and employability as part of the future of work. The chapter reiterates the impact of the COVID-19 pandemic on job insecurity and unemployment and the growing gap between the expectations of an employer and employees about career development and flexible work arrangements required to operate in a volatile, uncertain, complex, and ambiguous business and economic environment. To address such issues, the authors develop a conceptual framework that postulates the need for employees to develop a contemporary career attitude where they take responsibility and personal agency in their career decisions to improve their employability, career success, and sense of meaning in life, and for employers, to support employees to self-manage their careers by implementing effective learning practices, flexible work arrangements, and mentoring systems, which should result in success at both the personal and organizational level.

To this end, we, the editors, would like to thank the submitting authors for dedicating their effort and time to craft insightful material for this book, as well as the voluntary reviewers for their investment in supporting the authors to improve their work in a highly constructive and developmental manner.

Thank you and happy reading!
Weng Marc Lim
Surinderpal Kaur
Huey Fen Cheong

Section A

The impact of COVID-19 on business and economy

1 The quarantine economy

The case of COVID-19 and Malaysia

Weng Marc Lim

1.1 Introduction

The coronavirus disease 2019 (COVID-19) is a pandemic like no other. In particular, the COVID-19 pandemic has exhausted economies around the world in addition to the public health crisis that it has created, taking away many lives and infecting and causing suffering to many more. The seminal article on the history, lessons, and ways forward from the COVD-19 pandemic by Lim (2021b) highlighted that the COVID-19 pandemic is unlike the Spanish flu, which infected a third of the world's population and took away the lives of up to 100 million people in the early 1900s. Specifically, Lim (2021b) indicated that the COVID-19 pandemic occurred in an era where globalization has matured, and disruptive Fourth Industrial Revolution (IR 4.0) technologies are omnipresent, leading to a mix of positive (e.g., solutions delivered at a greater pace, as seen through the pandemic and its vaccines emerging in the same year) and negative (e.g., damaging shocks on economic and public health) impacts.

Of particular interest in this chapter is the economic impact of the COVID-19 pandemic in Malaysia. In particular, the COVID-19 pandemic has led to massive lockdowns around the world, including Malaysia, and thus resulting in an initial pause and then a reconfiguration of economic activities. This unprecedented phenomenon can be encapsulated through a concept that the chapter coins as *the quarantine economy.* Here, the initial pause refers to the temporary industry shutdowns that economies across the globe encountered when COVID-19 was declared as a pandemic by the World Health Organization, and it was during this shutdown that governments around the world limited the opening of the economy to only the industries that provide essential goods (e.g., grocery retailers) and services (e.g., healthcare and logistics providers). The initial pause was nonetheless quick, as governments reopened the economies gradually with new social practices (e.g., remote work, physical distancing,

DOI: 10.4324/9781003182740-1

visitor records) being enforced, thereby leading to a reconfiguration of how economic activities can be carried out during the pandemic.

In the academic and scientific landscape, the literature has not grown at a slower pace despite the COVID-19 pandemic. Instead, it has proliferated rapidly, as seen through the hundreds of thousands of search results that emerge from a Google Scholar search for "COVID-19" and "economy" in 2020, and thus indicating that the pandemic has largely served as an impetus rather than a barrier for new research. Yet, two shortcomings are apparent in the literature at the time of writing. First, research on COVID-19 and the economy, where business is prevalent, avail predominantly from the international perspective, as seen through the Web of Science review by Carracedo et al. (2021) and the Scopus review by Verma and Gustafsson (2020) on the topic in the *Journal of Business Research*. Though such a perspective is undeniably important, especially for theory development, its broad outlook may be too general to satisfy the appetite of stakeholders who wish to gain a contextual outlook, for example, a country-specific outlook (e.g., Malaysia). Second, though scarce research on COVID-19 and the economy relating to a country-specific outlook, particularly Malaysia, are available, they generally rely on piecemeal data (e.g., incomplete year) (e.g., Khalid, 2021; Lee et al., 2020). Though such research can be valuable for providing expeditious insights during the crisis, it cannot provide a stable evaluation of the crisis (e.g., a year-long perspective).

In line with the call by Lim and To (2021) to evaluate the economic impact of the COVID-19 pandemic using a year-long perspective, which they suggest is a pragmatic endeavour today given the availability of such data, this chapter aims to unpack the insights pertaining to the Malaysian economy in 2020, wherein the COVID-19 pandemic has had a significant impact. The insights presented herein are derived from secondary sources, which inform the critical review of the phenomenon under study. The outcome of this chapter is not meant to extend theory or result in novelty but rather to help readers gain a pragmatic understanding of the impact of the COVID-19 pandemic on the Malaysian economy. Such an understanding will also help readers to appreciate the subsequent chapters that focus on a variety of issues relating to business in the Malaysian economy as a result of the COVID-19 pandemic.

1.2 Methodology

This chapter adopts a critical review approach to research that is predicated on secondary data. In essence, many review approaches exist (e.g., critical, systematic, post-published) (Paul et al., 2021), but a critical review approach was chosen as it enables the present chapter to build on the systematic reviews by Carracedo et al. (2021) and Verma and Gustafsson (2020) and deal with the issues of concern—that is, insights on the quarantine economy from a Malaysian perspective—in a direct and straightforward way. The methodological decision is also in line with the recommendations of Paul et al. (2021) to pursue critical reviews for studies that do not focus entirely on academic literature, and that intend to resolve issues that are already known. The choice of using secondary data is also pragmatic given that such data are readily available and would complement the primary data that entail in the ensuing chapters. Specifically, the secondary data reported in this chapter consists of the economic data and events that transpired in Malaysia in 2020 and up to May 1, 2021, which were obtained from academic research, government agencies, and press releases and used to inform this critical review.

1.3 Findings

To combat the COVID-19 pandemic, the Government of Malaysia has implemented the 6R strategy of *Resolve*, *Resilient*, *Restart*, *Recovery*, *Revitalise*, and *Reform*. Figure 1.1 provides an illustration of the 6R

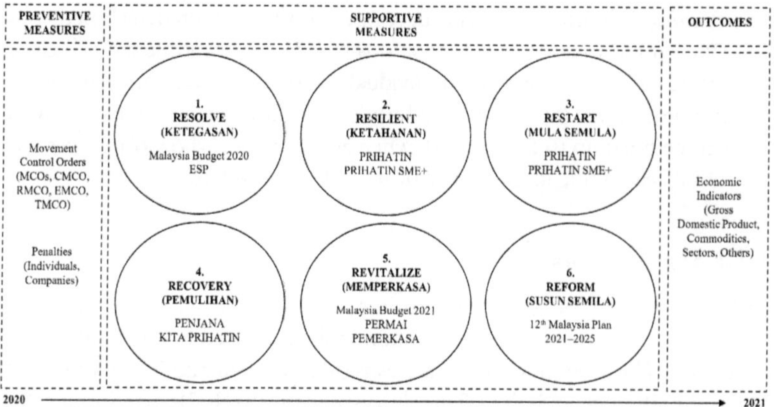

Figure 1.1 The 6R strategy to tackle the COVID-19 pandemic and revive the Malaysian economy

Abbreviations: MCO = movement control order. CMCO = conditional MCO. RMCO = recovery MCO. EMCO = enhanced MCO. TMCO = targeted MCO. ESP = Economic Stimulus Package. PRIHATIN = Pakej Rangsangan Ekonomi Prihatin Rakyat or Prihatin Rakyat Economic Stimulus Package. PRIHATIN SME+ = Additional PRIHATIN SME Economic Stimulus Package. PENJANA = Pelan Jana Semula Ekonomi Negara or National Economic Recovery Plan. KITA PRIHATIN = PRIHATIN Supplementary Initiative Package. PERMAI = Perlindungan Ekonomi dan Rakyat Malaysia or Malaysian Economic and Rakyat's Protection Assistance Package. PEMERKASA = Program Strategik Memperkasa Rakyat dan Ekonomi or Strategic Program to Empower the People and Economy. Illustration is a synthesis of myriad sections in this chapter.

strategy alongside the preventive and supportive measures that the government has implemented to tackle the COVID-19 pandemic and revive the Malaysian economy.

1.3.1 Preventive measures

The Government of Malaysia developed and implemented several preventive measures to manage the economic and public health concerns emerging from the COVID-19 pandemic. In particular, two categories of preventive measures are most prevalent:

1 *Movement control order* (*MCO*). The government developed and implemented five different MCOs, namely, MCO, conditional MCO (CMCO), recovery MCO (RMCO), enhanced MCO (EMCO), and targeted MCO (TMCO). The different MCOs reflect different restriction levels pertaining to interstate travel, formal and informal events, business and social activities, and dining access, among others. The regulations evolve over time, and thus, it is best to refer to the *Malaysian National Security Council* (*Majlis Keselamatan Negara Malaysia*) official website for the latest updates (https://www.mkn.gov.my).

2 *Penalties*. The government has developed and implemented the Emergency (Prevention and Control of Infectious Diseases) (Amendment) Ordinance 2021, which stipulates that individuals who violate the standard operating procedures (SOPs) imposed under the different variations of MCO can be fined up to RM10,000, whereas companies who violate the same can receive a fine up to RM50,000 (USD1 ≈ RM4.10).

1.3.2 Supportive measures

The Government of Malaysia introduced and implemented several supportive measures to cushion the economic shock caused by the COVID-19 pandemic. These supportive measures reside between the 2020 and 2021 Malaysian Budget and the 12th Malaysia Plan (2021–2025). Specifically, seven major economic stimulus packages (ESP) valued at a total of RM340 billion have been announced and implemented as of May 1, 2021:

1 *ESP* (*Economic Stimulus Package*). The ESP, which was announced on February 27, 2020, is worth RM20 billion and endeavours to bolster confidence, stimulate growth, and protect jobs. The ESP forms part of the next economic stimulus package as a result of a transition between prime ministers from (Tun Dr.) Mahathir Mohammad to (Tan Sri) Muhyiddin Yassin.

2 *PRIHATIN* (*Pakej Rangsangan Ekonomi Prihatin Rakyat* or *Prihatin Rakyat Economic Stimulus Package*). The PRIHATIN ESP, which was announced on March 27, 2020, is worth RM250 billion, with almost RM128 billion channelled to protect the welfare of the people, RM100 billion for supporting businesses, RM2 billion to strengthen the economy, and RM20 billion from the previous ESP. More information can be found at https://pre2020.treasury.gov.my/.
3 *PRIHATIN SME+* (*Additional PRIHATIN SME Economic Stimulus Package*). The PRIHATIN SME+ is a supplementary package to the PRIHATIN ESP aimed at assisting small and medium enterprises (SMEs) and micro-businesses. PRIHATIN SME+ was announced on April 6, 2020, and is valued at RM10 billion, which includes an additional RM7.9 billion for the Wage Subsidy Program and RM2.1 billion Special Prihatin Grants for all eligible SMEs and micro-businesses.
4 *PENJANA* (*Pelan Jana Semula Ekonomi Negara* or *National Economic Recovery Plan*). The PENJANA ESP, which was announced on June 5, 2020, consists of 40 initiatives worth RM35 billion and endeavours to empower people, propel business, and stimulate the economy (Table 1.1). More information can be found at https://penjana.treasury.gov.my.
5 *KITA PRIHATIN* (*PRIHATIN Supplementary Initiative Package*). The KITA PRIHATIN ESP, which was announced on September 23, 2020, is a supplementary package to PRIHATIN and PENJANA worth RM10 billion to bolster the country's economy in weathering the impact of COVID-19. The package includes RM7 billion for the Bantuan PRIHATIN Nasional (BPN) 2.0 one-off cash assistance to B40 and M40 households, RM2.4 billion for the Wage Subsidy Program 2.0, and RM600 million for Special Prihatin Grants for microentrepreneurs.
6 *PERMAI* (*Perlindungan Ekonomi dan Rakyat Malaysia* or *Malaysian Economic and People's Protection Assistance Package*). The PERMAI ESP, which was announced on January 18, 2021, comprises 22 initiatives worth RM15 billion and endeavours to combat the COVID-19 outbreak, safeguard the welfare of the people, and support business continuity (Table 1.2). More information can be found at https://belanjawan2021.treasury.gov.my/permai/index-en.html.
7 *PEMERKASA* (*Program Strategik Memperkasa Rakyat dan Ekonomi* or *Strategic Program to Empower the People and Economy*). The PEMERKASA ESP, which was announced on March 17, 2021, focuses on five areas to curtail the spread of COVID-19, drive economic recovery, strengthen national competitiveness, ensure regional and community inclusion, and transform the economy. The budget

Table 1.1 National economic recovery plan (PENJANA)

No.	*Initiative*	*Budget*
Thrust 1: Empowering people		
1	Wage Subsidy Program	RM5 billion
2	National Employment Services Job Portal Upgrade	Unspecified
3	Hiring and Training Assistance for Businesses	RM1.5 billion
4	Reskilling and Upskilling Programs	RM2 billion
5	Gig Economy Social Protection and Skilling	RM75 million
6	Flexible Work Arrangement Incentives	RM800 million
7	Child Care Subsidy	RM200 million
8	MY30 Public Transport Subsidy	RM200 million
9	Social Assistance Support for Vulnerable Groups	RM108 million
10	PeKa B40 Healthcare Support	RM50 million
11	Internet Connectivity for Education and Productivity	RM3 billion
Thrust 2: Propelling businesses		
12	Micros and SMEs E-commerce Campaign	RM70 million
13	"Shop Malaysia Online" for Online Consumption	RM70 million
14	Technical and Digital Adoption for SMEs and MTCs	RM700 million
15	MyAssist SME One-Stop Shop	RM5 million
16	PENJANA SME Financing (PSF)	RM2 billion
17	PENJANA Tourism Financing (PTF)	RM1 billion
18	PENJANA Microfinancing	RM400 million
19	Bumiputera Relief Financing	RM500 million
20	SME Go Scheme for Liquidity Support	RM1.6 billion
21	Accelerated Payment Terms for GLCs and Large Corporates' Supply Chain	Unspecified
22	Tax Relief for COVID-19-related Expenses	RM600 million
23	Financial Stress Support for Businesses	RM2.4 billion
24	Social Enterprises Elevation	RM10 million
25	Spurring Set Up of New Businesses	RM300 million
Thrust 3: Stimulating economy		
26	Dana PENJANA Nasional	RM1.2 billion
27	National Technology and Innovation Sandbox	RM100 million
28	Digitalization of Government Service Delivery	RM20 million
29	National "Buy Malaysia" Campaign	RM20 million
30	ePENJANA Credits in e-wallet	RM750 million
31	Incentives for Property Sector	RM1 billion
32	Tax Incentives for Purchase of Passenger Cars	RM897 million
33	Extended Service Hours in the New Normal	RM20 million
34	Malaysia as Attractive Horizon for Businesses	RM50 million
35	Tourism Sector Support	RM1.8 billion
36	Arts, Culture, Entertainment, Events and Exhibitions Sector Support	RM225 million

37	Agriculture and Food Sector Support	RM400 million
38	Commodity Sector Support	RM200 million
39	COVID-19 Temporary Measures Act	Unspecified
40	Sukuk Prihatin	RM500 million

Notes: COVID-19 = coronavirus disease 2019. GLCs = government-linked companies. MTCs = mid-tier companies. PeKa B40 = Penyertaan Skim Peduli Kesihatan Untuk Kumpulan B40 or Health Protection Scheme for B40 Income Group. PENJANA = Pelan Jana Semula Ekonomi Negara or National Economic Recovery Plan. SMEs = small and medium enterprises. More information at https://penjana.treasury.gov.my.

Table 1.2 Malaysian economic and people's protection assistance package (PERMAI)

No.	*Initiative*	*Budget*
Thrust 1: Combatting the COVID-19 outbreak		
1	National COVID-19 Vaccine Program	RM3 billion
2	Additional Funds for COVID-19 Supply for Frontliners	RM1 billion
3	Recruitment of Healthcare Personnel	RM150 million
4	Cooperation with Private Hospitals	RM100 million
Thrust 2: Safeguarding the welfare of the people		
5	Increase in JKM (Social Welfare) Budget from 2021 Budget	RM2.2 billion
6	Free 1GB Daily Internet Data	RM500 million
7	Flood-related Initiatives (Including NADMA)	RM250 million
8	Food Basket Program	RM50 million
9	Disaster Relief Network Matching Grant	RM25 million
Thrust 3: Supporting business continuity		
10	Wage Subsidy Program 3.0	RM1 billion
11	Bus/Taxi Hire Purchase Scheme	RM1 billion
12	Microcredit Scheme	RM1 billion
13	Permai Special Prihatin Grant	RM650 million
14	SME E-commerce Campaign and Shop Malaysia Online	RM300 million
15	One-off Assistance to Bus and Taxi Drivers	RM70 million
16	PERKESO for Riders (Full Coverage) from 2021 Budget	RM24 million
Thrusts 1–3		
17	Others (e.g., Tax Reliefs, Guarantees)	RM3.68 billion

Notes: COVID-19 = coronavirus disease 2019. JKM = Jabatan Kebajikan Masyarakat or Department of Social Welfare. NADMA = National Disaster Management Agency. PERKESO = Pertubuhan Keselamatan Sosial or Social Security Organisation. SME = small and medium enterprise. More information at https://belanjawan2021.treasury.gov.my/permai/index-en.html.

allocated for this ESP is RM20 billion, which includes an increase to RM5 billion from the RM3 billion announced for the National COVID-19 Vaccine Program, an increase to RM5 billion from the RM2.5 billion announced for small-scale projects, RM1.2b billion for one-off cash payments to laid-off workers from B40 and people earning RM1,000 and below, an additional allocation of RM500 million in microcredit financing for SMEs, RM300 million for PenjanaKerja by PERKESO to help in the reemployment of retrenched workers, and an additional allocation of RM700 million for Wage Subsidy Program 3.0, among others. More information can be found at http://belanjawan2021.treasury.gov.my/index.php/ms/pemerkasa.

1.3.3 Outcomes

The Government of Malaysia reports the progress of the implementation of the ESPs through the LAKSANA reports, and its 50th report was presented on April 22, 2021. More information can be found at https://pre2020.treasury.gov.my/.

Notwithstanding the infographics and informative insights presented in the LAKSANA reports, which essentially communicate the updates on the budget distributed for the support initiatives and the equivalent number of beneficiaries, the present chapter presents insights into the Malaysian economy through available yearly economic indicators for 2019 and 2020 (Table 1.3), which were manually computed based on the monthly and quarterly data compiled and made available by the Department of Statistics Malaysia. The indicators were segmented into four categories: gross domestic product (GDP), commodities, sector, and others. More information about the breakdown can be found at https://www.dosm.gov.my/.

In terms of *GDP*, which is the monetary value of all finished goods and services made in the country and thus a reflection of the estimated size of its economy and economic growth, Malaysia has experienced a decline of close to 5.6% or RM100 billion from RM1.4 trillion in 2019 to RM1.3 trillion in 2020. This figure may very well be higher without the RM340 billion worth of economic stimulus packages injected by the government into the quarantine economy.

In terms of *commodities*, which are the raw materials produced in the country, Malaysia's export has experienced a decline for rubber, oil palm products, palm oil, and liquefied natural gas, but a surge for palm kernel as well as crude petroleum and petroleum products in 2020 as compared to 2019. The prices of crude oil, however, have decreased by more than 30% within the same period, which has also contributed to the decline in GDP.

Table 1.3 Economic indicators of Malaysia in 2019 versus 2020

Indicators	Unit	2019	2020	2020
		Value	*Value*	*Annual percentage change (%)*
1.0 GROSS DOMESTIC PRODUCT				
1.1 Constant Prices	RM Million	1,421,454.0	1,342,026.9	- 5.59
2.0 COMMODITIES				
2.1 RUBBER				
2.1.1 Exports				
- Natural Rubber	Tonne	631,304.0	565,165.0	-10.48
2.2 OIL PALM				
2.2.1 Exports				
- Oil Palm Product	Tonne	27,879,175.0	26,655,394.0	- 4.39
- Palm Oil	Tonne	18,471,066.0	17,368,865.0	- 5.97
- Palm Kernel	Tonne	1,086,254.0	1,219,693.0	12.28
2.3 CRUDE PETROLEUM				
2.3.1 Prices				
- Crude Oil, Brent	USD/Barrel	256.1	169.2	- 33.93
- Crude Oil, WTI	USD/Barrel	228.1	157.2	- 31.08
2.3.2 Exports				
- Crude Petroleum	’000 Tonne	12,452,188.3	13,011,254.6	4.49
- Petroleum Products	’000 Tonne	28,133,641.0	34,680,000.9	23.27
2.3.3 Imports				
- Crude Petroleum	’000 Tonne	12,776,163.3	11,955,224.8	- 6.43
- Petroleum Products	’000 Tonne	31,266,863.6	37,225,429.3	19.06

(*Continued*)

Table 1.3 (Continued)

Indicators	*Unit*	*2019* *Value*	*2020* *Value*	*2020* *Annual percentage change (%)*
2.4 LIQUIFIED NATURAL GAS (LNG)				
2.4.1 Exports				
- Liquefied Natural Gas	'000 Tonne	25,498,445.5	24,458,188.2	-4.08
3.0 SECTOR				
3.1 MANUFACTURING				
3.1.1 Industrial Production Index	Point	480.5	467.6	- 2.68
3.1.2 Sales	RM '000	1,376,027,400.0	1,346,619,570.0	- 2.14
3.1.3 Exports	RM '000	840,585,598.1	847,663,951.0	0.84
3.1.4 Manufacturing Project				
- Investment				
a Projects Number	Number	988.0	741.0	- 25.00
b Projects Domestics	RM Million	28,840.7	25,505.5	- 11.56
c Projects Foreign	RM Million	53,891.8	39,295.8	- 27.08
d Total	RM Million	82,732.7	64,801.4	- 21.67
3.2 CONSTRUCTION				
3.2.1 Quarterly Construction	RM	146,371.7	117,918.1	- 19.44
3.2.2 Unit Price Index of Construction Materials 2015=100	Point	428.0	432.7	1.10
3.2.3 Issuance of Developer License, Sales Permit, and Housing Advertisement (New Permit)	Unit	1,124.0	797.0	- 29.09

	3.2.4	Issuance of Developer License, Sales Permit, and Housing Advertisement (Renewals Permit)	Unit	1,926.0	2,392.0	24.20
	3.2.5	**Prices**				
		- Steel	RM per Metric Tonne	9,523.7	9,528.8	0.05
		- Cement	RM per 50 Kg Bag	69.0	70.9	2.75
3.3	**MINING AND QUARRYING**					
	3.3.1	Mining Index (Base 2015 = 100)	Point	394.3	356.1	- 9.69
3.4	**UTILITIES**					
	3.4.1	**Electricity**				
		- Local Generation				
		a Public Installations	Million Kilowatt-Hours	166,233.6	159,032.0	- 4.33
		b Private Installations	Million Kilowatt-Hours	2,170.0	2,188.3	0.84
		- Local Consumption				
		a Industrial, Commercial and Mining	Million Kilowatt-Hours	116,368.8	106,311.6	- 8.64
		b Domestic and Public Lighting	Million Kilowatt-Hours	33,385.6	36,423.0	9.10
3.5	**SERVICES**					
	3.5.1	**Wholesale and Retail Trade**				
	3.5.2	**Volume Index**				
		- Wholesale Trade Index	Point	514.1	487.4	- 5.19
		- Retail Trade Index	Point	558.0	524.1	- 6.08
		- Motor Vehicle Index	Point	418.4	372.9	-10.87
	3.5.3	**Motor Vehicle**				
		- Vehicle Production				

(*Continued*)

Table 1.3 (Continued)

Indicators	*Unit*	*2019* *Value*	*2020* *Value*	*2020* *Annual percentage change (%)*
a Passenger	Unit	533,727.0	457,776.0	- 14.23
b Commercial	Unit	37,519.0	27,442.0	- 26.86
c Total	Unit	571,246.0	485,218.0	- 15.06
- Vehicle Sales				
a Passenger	Unit	550,178.0	473,843.0	- 13.87
b Commercial	Unit	54,106.0	48,248.0	- 10.83
c Total	Unit	604,284.0	522,091.0	- 13.60
- New Vehicles Registration	Number	1,373,198.0	1,163,366.0	-15.28
3.5.4 Tourism				
- Index of Services	Point	508.6	255.2	- 49.82
- Tourist Arrivals	Number	26,100,784.0	4,299,419.0	- 83.53
3.5.5 Transport				
- Index of Services	Point	502.0	388.9	- 22.53
3.5.6 Information and Communication				
- Index of Services	Point	540.0	571.1	5.76
- Penetration Rate				
a Mobile Cellular per 100 Inhabitants	%	533.4	266.4	- 50.06
b Fixed Telephone per 100 Inhabitants	%	78.6	19.8	- 74.81
c Broadband per 100 Inhabitants	%	517.1	127.4	- 75.36

3.5.7	**Finance**				
	- Index of Services	Point	462.7	473.5	2.33
I	**Money Supply**				
	- M1	RM Million	1,746,267.7	1,986,816.3	13.78
	- M2	RM Million	7,644,146.7	8,045,683.9	5.25
	- M3	RM Million	7,688,855.8	8,067,941.3	4.93
II	**Total Loans in Banking System**	RM Million	6,962,496.1	7,238,780.4	3.97
	- Commercial Banks	RM Million	4,563,850.6	4,648,998.1	1.87
	- Islamic Banks	RM Million	2,371,671.4	2,561,968.9	8.02
	- Merchant Banks	RM Million	26,974.3	27,813.4	3.11
III	**Total Deposits Banking System (Fixed and Savings Deposits)**	RM Million	7,893,099.3	8,221,789.6	4.16
	- Commercial Banks	RM Million	5,410,801.2	5,617,882.0	3.83
	- Islamic Banks	RM Million	2,384,042.6	2,514,896.9	5.49
	- Merchant Banks	RM Million	98,255.4	89,010.5	- 9.41
IV	**Fixed Deposits, Tawarruq Fixed Deposits, Special and General Investment Deposits**	RM Million	4,010,320.4	3,934,568.6	- 1.89
	- Commercial Banks	RM Million	2,358,475.1	2,339,357.7	- 0.81
	- Islamic Banks	RM Million	1,589,482.5	1,536,320.6	- 3.34
	- Merchant Banks	RM Million	62,362.9	58,890.4	- 5.57
V	**Savings Deposits**	RM Million	663,664.7	801,078.2	20.71
	- Commercial Banks	RM Million	487,486.0	576,305.5	18.22
	- Islamic Banks	RM Million	176,178.7	224,772.8	27.58
VI	**Overnight Policy Rate (OPR)**	Basis Point	12.3	8.0	- 34.96
VII	**Average Lending Rate CFM**				
	- Commercial Banks	%	19.5	15.8	- 18.97
	- Islamic Banks	%	21.1	17.8	- 15.64
	- Merchant Banks	%	25.9	24.3	- 6.18

(Continued)

Table 1.3 (Continued)

	Indicators	Unit	2019	2020	2020
			Value	*Value*	*Annual percentage change (%)*
VIII	**Base Lending Rate (BLR) Commercial Banks**	%	27.1	23.3	- 14.02
IX	**Base Financing Rate (BFR) Islamic Banks**	%	27.5	23.6	- 14.18
X	**Savings Deposits Interest Rate**				
	- Commercial Banks	%	4.1	2.5	- 39.02
	- Islamic Banks	%	3.0	1.8	- 40.00
XI	**Loans Approved by Sector**				
	- Primary Agriculture	RM Million	9,566.3	4,595.2	- 51.96
	- Mining and Quarrying	RM Million	3,129.6	1,930.2	- 38.32
	- Manufacturing	RM Million	36,733.5	31,202.9	- 15.06
	- Services	RM Million	86,254.1	85,364.9	- 1.03
	- Construction	RM Million	28,442.7	21,196.5	- 25.48
	- Real Estates	RM Million	25,177.3	16,867.3	- 33.01
	- Household Sector	RM Million	218,536.4	189,568.0	- 13.26
	- Other Sectors	RM Million	2,468.2	2,823.7	14.40
	- Total	RM Million	410,308.1	353,548.6	- 13.83
XII	**Loans Disbursed by Sector**				
	- Primary Agriculture	RM Million	44,402.1	38,482.8	- 13.33
	- Mining and Quarrying	RM Million	8,065.7	5,847.2	- 27.51
	- Manufacturing	RM Million	258,602.4	251,592.5	- 2.71

	- Services	RM Million	391,907.6	390,699.0	- 0.31
	- Construction	RM Million	90,047.4	77,778.7	- 13.62
	- Real Estates	RM Million	58,099.4	44,087.7	- 24.12
	- Foreign	RM Million	346,010.2	319,477.3	- 7.67
	- Other Sectors	RM Million	33,895.6	37,098.6	9.45
	- Total	RM Million	1,231,030.2	1,165,063.8	- 5.36
	XIII Loans Disbursed by Purpose				
	- Purchase of Passenger Cars	RM Million	42,583.6	38,275.8	- 10.12
	- Personal Uses	RM Million	35,011.2	31,763.4	- 9.28
	- Credit Cards	RM Million	150,702.8	133,212.9	- 11.61
	- Purchase of Consumer Durable Goods	RM Million	26.1	26.7	2.30
	- Loan Disbursed to Household Sector	RM Million	346,010.2	319,477.3	- 7.67
	XIV Outstanding Loans to the Construction Sector	RM Million	371,500.1	374,194.5	0.73
3.5.8	**Owner Occupied Dwelling**				
	- Loan Approved (for Residential)	RM Million	112,571.0	93,124.0	- 17.28
	- Loan Disbursed (for Residential)	RM Million	92,524.0	82,312.4	- 11.04
3.5.9	**Real Estate**				
	- Index of Services	Point	489.0	401.7	- 17.85
3.5.10	**Health**				
	- Index of Services – Private Health	Point	498.0	464.7	- 6.69
3.5.11	**Education**				
	- Index of Services – Private Education	Point	500.1	462.8	- 7.46

(*Continued*)

Table 1.3 (Continued)

Indicators	*Unit*	*2019* *Value*	*2020* *Value*	*2020* *Annual percentage change (%)*
4.0 OTHERS				
4.1 LABOUR				
4.1.1 Labour Supply				
- Working Age (15–64)	('000)	90,873.7	92,385.1	1.66
- Labour Force	('000)	62,566.6	63,228.5	1.06
i Employed	('000)	60,505.0	60,384.4	- 0.20
ii Unemployed	('000)	2,061.5	2,844.1	37.96
a Actively Unemployed	('000)	1,490.7	2,068.5	38.76
b Inactively Unemployed	('000)	570.8	775.6	35.88
- Outside Labour Force	('000)	28,307.1	29,156.6	3.00
- Labour Force Participation Rate	%	68.9	68.5	- 0.58
- Unemployment Rate	%	3.3	4.5	36.36
4.1.2 Labour Demand		ww		
- Jobs	('000)	34,481.6	33,879.1	- 1.75
- Filled Jobs	('000)	33,662.6	33,188.5	- 1.41
- Rate	%	97.7	98.0	0.31
- Vacancies	('000)	819.0	690.7	- 15.67
- Rate	%	2.4	2.0	- 16.67
- Jobs Created	('000)	104.0	73.3	- 29.52

4.1.3	**Labour Productivity**				
	- Value Added per Hour Worked	RM	162.3	169.0	4.13
	i By Economic Activity				
	a Agriculture	RM	103.0	105.3	2.23
	b Mining and Quarrying	RM	2,201.6	2,200.4	- 0.05
	c Manufacturing	RM	206.8	222.6	7.64
	d Construction	RM	75.8	71.9	- 5.15
	e Services	RM	154.1	160.1	3.89
	- Value Added per Employment	RM	93,958.0	88,841.0	- 5.45
	ii By Economic Activity				
	a Agriculture	RM	54,195.0	53,224.0	- 1.79
	b Mining and Quarrying	RM	1,349,965.0	1,242,932.0	- 7.93
	c Manufacturing	RM	123,881.0	120,604.0	- 2.65
	d Construction	RM	45,304.0	38,068.0	- 15.97
	e Services	RM	89,490.0	84,121.0	- 6.00
4.1.4	**Share of Registered Candidates by Qualification**				
	- Non-Tertiary	%	17.0	17.0	0.00
	- Tertiary	%	75.5	75.0	- 0.66
	- Postgraduate	%	8.0	7.5	- 6.25
4.1.5	**Share of Registered Candidates by Year of Experience**				
	- <1 year	%	27.0	26.0	- 3.70
	- 1–4 years	%	13.5	12.0	- 11.11
	- 5–9 years	%	22.0	22.0	0.00
	- 10–14 years	%	16.0	16.3	1.88
	- 15–19 years	%	10.8	11.3	4.63
	- =>20 years	%	11.3	14.5	28.32

(Continued)

Table 1.3 (Continued)

Indicators		Unit	2019 Value	2020 Value	2020 Annual percentage change (%)
4.2	**STOCK MARKET**				
4.2.1	Kuala Lumpur Composite Index	Point	6,488.4	5,983.9	- 7.78
4.2.2	Value Traded	RM Billion	525.3	1,068.0	103.31
4.3	**EXCHANGE RATE**				
4.3.1	USD – U.S. Dollar	RM per Unit	16.6	16.8	1.20
4.3.2	GBP – U.K. Pound	RM per Unit	21.2	21.6	1.89
4.3.3	SDR – Special Drawing Right	RM per Unit	22.9	23.4	2.18
4.3.4	SGD – Singapore Dollar	RM per Unit	12.1	12.2	0.83
4.3.5	EUR – EURO	RM per Unit	18.6	19.2	3.23
4.3.6	CHF – Swiss Franc	RM per 100 Units	1,667.6	1,791.4	7.42
4.3.7	JPY – Japanese Yen	RM per 100 Units	15.2	15.8	3.95
4.3.8	HKD – Hong Kong Dollar	RM per 100 Units	211.5	216.8	2.51

Notes: The table consists of available short-term economic indicators that the author computed based on the monthly and quarterly indicators compiled and reported by the Department of Statistics Malaysia. More information at https://www.dosm.gov.my/.

In terms of *sectors*, which represent groupings of similar and related economic activities, Malaysia has generally experienced a decline in its biggest sectors such as manufacturing, construction, mining and quarrying, utilities, and services in 2020 as compared to 2019. However, some upshots were observed within the same period, particularly in the utility sector, where private consumption of electricity has increased, which may be attributed to remote work that Malaysians had to undertake in their private residences during the COVID-19 pandemic. In addition, existing developers in the construction industry also remained optimistic, as seen through the increase in permit renewals, despite the increase in the cost of cement and steel and the overall price index of construction materials. Noteworthily, the mixed trends observed in the financial sector suggest that the money that the government has allocated through the various grants and payments budgeted in the economic stimulus packages have indeed been distributed, as seen through the increase in total deposits and loans, and thus, the supply of money in the economy, as seen through the increase in saving deposits. Finally, the education, health, and real estate sectors are also badly affected, as seen by the 6–18% decline in their respective service indices.

In terms of other economic indicators, Malaysia has experienced an increase in its labour supply (+1.66%), but unfortunately, much of the human capital in the *labour market* remain unemployed, as seen through the increase in the unemployment rate from 3.3% in 2019 to 4.5% in 2020, and the decrease in labour force participation rate from 68.9% to 68.5% within the same period. Most jobs available are filled (98%), and thus, the issues associated with unemployment can be attributed to a reduction in jobs available (–1.75%), created (–29.52%), and vacant (–16.67%). Nonetheless, it is important to note that the jobs available and created in Malaysia have historically been much lower than the labour supply, and the COVID-19 pandemic has simply amplified this persistent problem. Yet, labour productivity in some of the biggest sectors such as agriculture (+4.13%), manufacturing (+7.64%), and services (+3.89%) have improved, indicating that Malaysians who still have a job have worked more during than before the COVID-19 pandemic. The *stock market* remains highly active during the pandemic, as seen through the increase in the value of stocks traded (+103.31%), though the composite index has taken a hit (–7.78%), thereby indicating overall lower investor confidence during the COVID-19 pandemic. Similarly, the Malaysian Ringgit has shrunk against all major *currencies*, though such depreciation can benefit the country by propelling its exports, as mentioned previously.

1.4 Conclusion

To this end, this chapter makes clear that the quarantine economy in Malaysia has experienced both positive and negative impacts as a result of the COVID-19 pandemic. The Government of Malaysia has also continuously injected funds into the Malaysian economy through various economic stimuli and supplementary packages to cushion the negative impacts of the COVID-19 pandemic. Though some commodities and sectors have benefitted, others have not, thus indicating a need for a targeted rather than a one-size-fits-all intervention. The issue of unemployment continues to be a major concern, and the low availability of jobs and job creation remain as problems that have been magnified during the COVID-19 pandemic, which suggest that entrepreneurship and foreign direct investment will need to proliferate in order to match the supply of human capital in the labour market.

Nonetheless, this chapter is not without limitations. Though this chapter offers evidence on the distribution of allocation monies to beneficiaries in the economy, as seen through the surge in the economic indicators in the finance sector, the extent to which the monies have been distributed (e.g., partially, fully) and its equivalent reach to intended beneficiaries will need additional investigation. Such an endeavour rests primarily with government agencies as it is too big a task for any scholar, though proxies can also be deployed (e.g., sampling, surveys). Moreover, this chapter adopts a practice rather than a scholarly perspective to the investigation, and thus, future research is encouraged to dive deeper into the academic research pertaining to the economic impact of the COVID-19 pandemic in Malaysia. For example, future research can dive deeper into the economic stimulus packages to examine their impact on the well-being of the targeted beneficiaries, wherein the before and after conditions can be created and tested causally regardless of whether secondary or primary data is used (Lim, 2021a). If research relying on primary data is pursued, then behavioural control can also be considered, wherein the relationship between the degree to which allocations are received and the degree to which targeted behavioural performance is enacted can be investigated, with a scrutiny of the control factors that enable or inhibit behavioural performance (Lim and Weissmann, 2021). Similar reviews using other reviews approaches, such as bibliometric reviews (Donthu et al., 2021), rapid reviews (Lim, 2021c), and systematic literature reviews (Paul et al., 2021), are also highly encouraged as they can be used to source for context-specific (e.g., country, sector) insights from the extant literature, thereby building on the insights from this chapter as well as the next chapters in this book.

Summary

- The concept of the quarantine economy is introduced and explained.
- The preventive and supportive measures in the quarantine economy are presented.
- The economic impact of the COVID-19 pandemic on the Malaysian economy is delineated.

References

Carracedo, P., Puertas, R., & Marti, L. (2021). Research lines on the impact of the COVID-19 pandemic on business: A text mining analysis. *Journal of Business Research*, *132*, 586–593. https://doi.org/10.1016/j.jbusres.2020.11.043

Donthu, N., Kumar, S., Mukherjee, D., Pandey, N., & Lim, W. M. (2021). How to conduct a bibliometric analysis: An overview and guidelines. *Journal of Business Research*, *133*, 285–296. https://doi.org/10.1016/j.jbusres.2021.04.070

Khalid, M. A. (2021). Covid-19: Malaysia experience and key lessons. *Asian Economic Papers*, *20*(2), 73–95. https://doi.org/10.1162/asep_a_00801

Lee, K. Y. M., Jais, M., & Chan, C. W. (2020). Impact of COVID-19: Evidence from Malaysian stock market. *International Journal of Business and Society*, *21*(2), 607–628.

Lim, W. M. (2021a). Conditional recipes for predicting impacts and prescribing solutions for externalities: The case of COVID-19 and tourism. *Tourism Recreation Research*, *46*(2), 314–318. https://doi.org/10.1080/02508281.2021.1881708

Lim, W. M. (2021b). History, lessons, and ways forward from the COVID-19 pandemic. *International Journal of Quality and Innovation*, *5*(2), 101–108.

Lim, W. M. (2021c). Toward an agency and reactance theory of crowding: Insights from COVID-19 and the tourism industry. *Journal of Consumer Behaviour* (in press). https://doi.org/10.1002/cb.1948

Lim, W. M., & To, W. M. (2021). The economic impact of a global pandemic on the tourism economy: The case of COVID-19 and Macao's destination-and gambling-dependent economy. *Current Issues in Tourism* (in press). https://doi.org/10.1080/13683500.2021.1910218

Lim, W. M., & Weissmann, M. A. (2021). Toward a theory of behavioral control. *Journal of Strategic Marketing* (in press). https://doi.org/10.1080/0965254X.2021.1890190

Paul, J., Lim, W. M., O'Cass, A., Hao, A. W., & Bresciani, S. (2021). Scientific Procedures and Rationales for Systematic Literature Reviews (SPAR-4-SLR). *International Journal of Consumer Studies* (in press). https://doi.org/10.1111/ijcs.12695

Verma, S., & Gustafsson, A. (2020). Investigating the emerging COVID-19 research trends in the field of business and management: A bibliometric analysis approach. *Journal of Business Research*, *118*, 253–261. https://doi.org/10.1016/j.jbusres.2020.06.057

2 The impact of COVID-19 on agriculture in Malaysia

Insights from mixed methods

Firuza Begham Mustafa

2.1 Introduction

The novel coronavirus (COVID-19) earlier was referred to as a novel coronavirus, a severe acute coronavirus syndrome (SARS-CoV-2). The COVID-19 outbreak started in Wuhan, Hubei Province, China, and quickly spread to almost all the countries. The World Health Organization (WHO) had officially declared COVID-19 as a global pandemic. The report showed that 221 countries and territories of the world had recorded a total of 130,801,304 confirmed cases of the COVID-19 and a death toll of 2,850,147 deaths, while Malaysia has recorded 347,972 6,855 confirmed cases and 1,283 deaths (Worldometer, Saturday, April 3, 2021).

In the efforts to contain the spread of the COVID-19 pandemic, the Malaysian government had embarked on the Movement Control Order (MCO) and Conditional Movement Control Order (CMCO) to impose travel restrictions and movement controls. The agricultural sector is one of the most directly affected by the movement's control order. The pandemic has a significant impact on Malaysia's agricultural industry, particularly on the food sector, as the country imports 40% of its consumption from different countries. Smallholder farmers experience the problem of dumping agricultural products due to the closure of several supporting sectors such as transportation, retails, and logistics. Lack of cash reserves has worsened the impact as their earnings rely on daily sales revenue. The question is, what are the implications of the COVID-19 pandemic on the agriculture food production system and practices in Malaysia? The impact of the pandemic on the agricultural food supply system, especially on smallholder farmers. The onset of COVID-19 posed a wake-up call for those who had previously believed that food accessibility and affordability came naturally in Malaysia. Food security in Malaysia is jeopardized as a result of the MCO's introduction.

DOI: 10.4324/9781003182740-2

The phrase "sustainable agriculture" refers to a farm's ability to produce food continuously without causing permanent damage to the health of the ecosystem. Agriculture is one of the most important sectors in human development and is related to food security. The objective of this research is to analyse the relationships between agriculture and food security and how these relationships are being affected by events related to the disease of COVID-19. The agricultural sector is one of the most directly affected by the movement's control order due to COVID-19 pandemic outbreaks, which connect farm production to the consumer.

This study aimed to examine the effects of the COVID-19 pandemic on the system and practices of agricultural food production. This paper will answer a series of questions:

1 What is the impact of COVID-19 on the agriculture sector in Malaysia?
2 What is the impact of COVID-19 on farmers?
3 What is the impact of COVID-19 on production? sales? income?
4 What is the impact of COVID-19 on inputs-labour, machine?
5 What is the strategy? Suggestions and recommendations to eliminate or minimize the impacts.

The study was intended to explore the impact of COVID-19 on the agriculture sector in Malaysia and what is the impact of COVID-19 on the farmers. The research finding may help us to understand more about the impact of COVID-19 on agriculture production and revenue. The research finding may also be of substantial help to government agencies and the Ministry of Agriculture as it will help to address the challenges that impeded the agriculture sector. Finally, the study was intended to provide some strategy and plan to improve agriculture in future planning and long-term strategic plan for farmers and the agriculture sector.

2.2 Method

The study aims to employ quantitative and qualitative information to assess COVID-19 impact on agriculture. The primary data collection for this study is divided into two phases; the first phase involved the collection of general information through a pilot study and field observation. The second phase covered the survey to the farmers and agriculture extension service. The primary data sourced through focus group discussions and informal meetings. The secondary data used include research papers and publications on the subject, government and international agency reports and publications, relevant literature on the subject matter in news, social media, and other publications. Unfortunately, the methodology of the research has changed dramatically due to the second lockdown in Malaysia, better known as MCO 2.0, which started from January 13, 2021 to various end dates across states according to their COVID-19 situation. The primary data collection, such as interviews, surveys, focus group discussion, and in-depth interviews, were cancelled.

This study was carried out from September 2020 to April 2021. A simple, informal interview online was held on November–December, 2020 to confirm research objectives. Farmers were selected based on willingness to participate in the research and also accessibility. The data was collected online to maintain social distancing and minimize any potential risks. The secondary data is a major source of information for this research. Data included research papers and publications on the subject, government and international agency reports and publications, relevant literature on the subject matter in news, social media, and other publications.

2.3 Findings

The enforcement of the Movement Control Order (MCO) as a preventive measure by the federal government of Malaysia in response to the COVID-19 pandemic in the country on March 18, 2020 has caused many implications to the agriculture sector.

2.3.1 Impact on agriculture operation

2.3.1.1 Operation

Malaysian agriculture system is dependent on many external resources such as technology, capital, and inputs. Farming activity retarded as the production inputs such as pesticide, fertilizer, seedling, feeding material, machinery is not available in the local market as the country border is closed. Malaysia depends on imported inputs in the agriculture sector. Industries such as poultry farms depend on imported maize, bran, and pellets as feeding material have significantly disturbed during the MCO.

Farmers' access to essential intermediate inputs such as pesticides, fungicides, herbicides, fertilizers, and other plant and seed nutrients could also be affected by the COVID-19 pandemic (OECD 2020). Pesticides, which are scarce and costly, can affect crop yields and development, particularly in developing countries. Closing borders or halting cross-border seed movement may be dangerous.

Farmers may have more difficulties receiving inputs as a result of new limits on the transportation of people and goods. Agriculture input demand dropped precipitously and only eventually resumed after the production plants were shut down as a result of the epidemic.

2.3.1.2 Labour

Globally, there are an estimated 272 million international migrants, with migrant workers accounting for two-thirds (164 million). While the vast majority (68%) of migrant workers seek jobs in high-income countries, a significant proportion (28%) works in middle-income countries such as Malaysia (Fair Labor Association, 2020).

Malaysia's agriculture sector is heavily dependent on foreign workers. Restrictions on the movement of people especially affect foreign workers and result in labour shortages on the farms. The migrant workers constitute up to 30% of the labour force. Current estimates on migrant workers vary, ranging as low as 3 million to 5.5 million, comprising of both documented migrant workers (about 2.2 million as of 2016) and undocumented migrant workers (1–3.5 million). Documented migrant workers are those with a valid passport and working permit, and undocumented are referred to as those without it. In the palm sector specifically, about 80% (352,330) of the total 451,507 workers in 2015 were documented, migrant workers. Of those, 80–90% were Indonesian citizens working mainly as fresh fruit bunch harvesters and collectors. These numbers do not include workers who are employed in the palm mills and refineries. While the hiring of undocumented migrant workers is not uncommon in the palm plantation sector, no official estimate can best indicate their number. In Sabah, the 2019 Regularization Program, which aims to legalize undocumented workers' immigration and employment status, registered over 123,575 undocumented Indonesian and Filipino workers in the plantation sector. Other migrant workers employed in the plantations, especially in West Malaysia (Peninsular Malaysia), include workers from Bangladesh, India, and Nepal (Fair Labor Association, 2020).

Labour shortages in agricultural sectors are being exacerbated by restrictions on cross-border mobility and lockdowns in many countries, particularly those labour-intensive productions (OECD 2020). The situation worsens as the disease progresses, making movement restrictions more and more stringent, causing labour shortages for the harvest, or difficulties for farmers to bring their products to market (Siche, 2020). This has an effect on the crops, livestock, and fishery sub-sectors, especially the labour-intensive ones, and its impact is felt across the agriculture value chain, impacting food supply and consumer prices. Shortage of labour could lead to production losses and shortages in the market. In many countries, in the European Union, the travel bans within the country have significantly reduced the available workforce for the fruits and vegetable sector in European countries (OECD 2020).

A lack of workers and logistical challenges are key issues that need to be addressed to strengthen the agriculture sector against the COVID-19 pandemic; the labour shortage and disruption of supplies were becoming the main challenges in local food production. There was a shortage of labours, and farmers are unable to harvest the products due to the movement control order. Therefore, many agricultural products are spoilt and wasted away.

The available workforce has also been reduced as a result of rising infection rates and unemployment, as well as lockdowns, even in critical industries. In addition to disrupting supply, infections in processing facilities have resulted in lower farm demand.

2.3.1.3 Inputs

The COVID-19 pandemic can also impact farmer's access to critical intermediate inputs such as pesticides, fungicides, herbicides, fertilizers, and other plant and crop nutrients. Inputs such as pesticides, which are scarce and expensive, may have an impact on yields and crop production, particularly in developing countries. Closing borders or slowing transboundary agriculture inputs movement could be detrimental. The farmers may have greater trouble accessing inputs due to additional constraints on the movement of people and products. The agriculture inputs production fell sharply and only gradually resumed after the production plants were shut down following the outbreak.

Farmers may have more difficulties receiving inputs as a result of new limits on the transportation of people and goods. Agriculture input demand dropped precipitously and only eventually resumed after the production plants were shut down as a result of the epidemic.

The key cause of the disturbances is a lack of raw materials, specifically an insufficient supply of feed to livestock farmers. Although such shortages have affected approximately 60% of the agricultural enterprises, they are most serious in the livestock farming field, where feed shortages mean that animals and poultry may starve to death. The industry faces a crisis that could lead to more price spikes. The spread of COVID-19 impacts had reduced the demand for chicken eggs while the bran cost, namely, imported maize and soya, had risen by about 30% (Rashidah Abd Rahim 2020).

2.3.1.4 Output

Surpluses are accumulating in many agricultural products due to disruptions downstream from the plant, putting a strain on storage facilities and, in the case of high perishables, growing food losses. Agriculture output abandoned and mass wastages in agriculture products such as vegetables, flowers, dairy milk, eggs, etc. Farmers and agribusiness operators, who have limited possession of downstream facilities, have struggled to find buyers. Demand side declines are compounding supply side disruptions for some goods. These factors are putting a strain on farm incomes. Furthermore, reduced off-farm income could compound those farm household income losses (OECD 2020).

Lockdowns and restrictions on individuals' mobility also affect food safety and quality controls, including those required for trade facilitation, such as goods physical inspections to certify compliance with health and plant health requirements inspection and check (OECD 2020).

The local news portal reported that restrictions on traffic and market operating hours under the MCO have adversely affected the supply chain for vegetables and raw produce. There have also been reports of vegetable farmers in Cameron Highlands throwing away their produce because of logistical issues (Supriya, 2020).

2.3.2 *Impact on food supply*

All countries, including main food exporters that produce much more food than they eat, depend on imports for at least some of their food intake. The country with the most autarky practices, such as North Korea, also imports food and accepts foreign food aid (FAO, 2015). Malaysia's global agricultural trade reached $43.5 billion in 2019, with exports of $25 billion and imports of $18.3 billion. Palm oil is the dominant export and the leading markets over the past several years for this Malaysian product include India, the European Union, China, Pakistan, and the United States. Thailand, Indonesia, and China are the top suppliers of agricultural products to Malaysia, with the United States ranked 5th in 2019. Despite the agricultural trade surplus with the world of $6.7 billion, Malaysia nonetheless still heavily relies on imports for many key products, including wheat, rice, protein meal, dairy products, beef, and most deciduous and citrus fruits (USDA Foreign Agricultural Service Malaysia, 2020) (Figure 2.1). Pandemic COVID-19 has disturbed the international agriculture trade and food supply, especially when all the border and international port is closed.

Measures to prevent the spread of the COVID-19 cause transport and logistics services from being delayed and disrupted. The congestion and delay resulting from border closures and additional procedures and checks affected the transit of goods. Social distancing requirements, for instance, have reduced the number of border import and export inspectors and increased the customs clearance time.

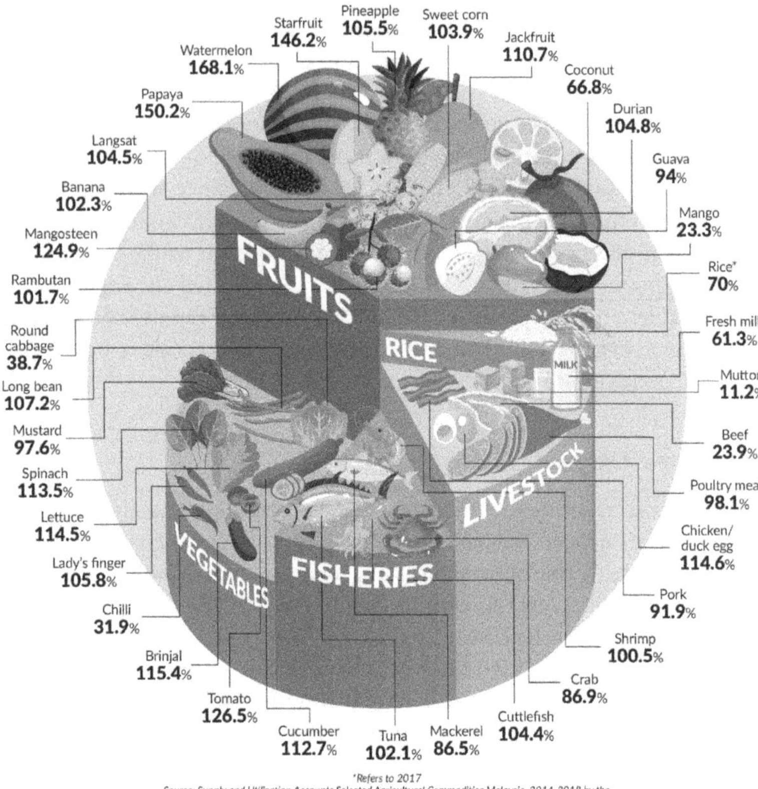

Figure 2.1 Self-sufficient ratio for selected agriculture commodities in Malaysia
Source: Retrieved from "Beefing up food security" by Dina Murad (2020), *The Star.*

Port closures can trigger problems as shipments must be moved from one port to another or a separate importing country entirely. When the virus hit, many cargo containers were in Chinese ports, and movement restrictions contributed to a deficiency in container prices that grew. This has also had flow-on impacts on freight prices and traffic levels. Food security is a measure of the steady availability of food, ideally healthy and nutritious food, to the population (Chin, 2020).

2.3.3 Changes in markets

This significant shift in the composition and, for some commodities, the level of demand will put pressure on entire value chains. Manufacturers are adjusting production and distribution, for example, to shift from producing bulk items for food service to producing smaller packages for home use. Some, on the other hand, will struggle to keep their businesses afloat. Perishables industries are more likely to be impacted than cereals and prepared foods markets. Social distancing practices and new norms for workers in agriculture processing plants such as grading and packaging the fruits, flowers, vegetables, and livestock products increasing the production cost and time.

The establishment of airlines and the increasing international freight costs as a result of lower trade volumes and the lack of commercial passenger flies cause significant difficulties in exporting high-value perishable food products, including marine, fruits, flowers, and vegetable products. There are reports that air freight costs between China and North America have increased by around 30% following travel bans and over 60% in some major routes across Europe and North America.

According to Kumar et al. (2021), the most significant knocks from the lockdown period have affected farming systems and value chains include:

a Immobility of agriculture workers;
b Insufficient storage capacity;
c Transportation and distribution difficulties;
d Inadequate supply of agricultural produce to meet demand.

2.4 Conclusion

The impact of COVID-19 on Malaysia's agriculture sector revolves around two major aspects: (i) impact on agriculture operation and (ii) impact on food supply. The COVID-19-induced pandemic disturbs the whole food system, from the primary supply to the final demand. The impacts in the agriculture and food supply include unemployment, poverty, and shrinkages in the overall economic activity.

What policies are needed to address these problems? More than any other industries, agricultural enterprises, and particularly those in the livestock farming sector, say they prefer rent reductions, financing support, and especially forced certification. Our survey makes it clear that apart from the above options, a simpler and more direct demand often expressed by the entrepreneurs is that the lockdown is ended. The Chinese government has already rolled out a series of pertinent measures, including opening a green channel for feed, to effectively stabilize agricultural production. However, this has not yet been implemented in all areas. While all relief efforts are important, it is even more urgent that these measures be implemented at the grassroots level. While maintaining effective control of the epidemic, it should be of the greatest importance to encourage enterprises in rural areas to return to work (Zhang, 2020).

Getting the food where it is required would need a stable supply chain that can respond to customer demand changes and adapt to supply restrictions resulting from COVID-19 actions. Though there are many unknowns and the situation is constantly changing, previous crises have provided insight into certain steps that policymakers can take to reduce COVID-19's effects on the food system and sustainability.

Food security is regarded as a chain and management problem; both the public and private sectors will benefit from COVID-19's expertise in rethinking how food production and use can be rendered more sustainable. The COVID-19 pandemic affected the agricultural supply chain, triggering labour restrictions and transportation of farm inputs and produce, as well as a rise in food prices due to the competitive economy and a shift in customer behaviour.

The recommendations strategy to activate food supply, food security, and sustainability according to the category:

a **Community**
   1 Urban agriculture
   Engaging in urban agriculture initiatives at the community and household levels, as well as promoting the local ability for self-sufficiency through well-planned local food production networks.
   2 Consumerism
   At the consumer and household level, awareness regarding balanced diets and behaviours, nutritious and high-micronutrient agricultural products, food processing and storage methods, and waste management strategies must be widely disseminated through different awareness channels.

b **Farmers**
   1 Farmers support system
   Smallholder farmers should be offered an induction to significant contraptions and advances. These can join amazing seeds, fertilizers, and sufficient developing stuff. Taking assessments, for instance, safe work practices and giving protective equipment for farmers, can decrease the spread of COVID-19 and advance food creation.
   2 Agri-food E-business
   Empowering web business in agri-business is another approach to take, as this supports trade, lessens transportation risks and allows induction to the market. Plan actions to help small and medium

industries in the agri-business territory to sell their things on electronic platforms.

3 Agri-entrepreneurs
Encouraging all sectors' participation in agri-entrepreneurs. Particularly the youth and women, through several systematic education and mentorship programs with well-thought-out and sustained incentives and innovative training modalities and backed with social safety net systems will be instrumental in sustaining these efforts.

c **Government and agencies**

1 Public-private associations
Public-private affiliations and interests in existing country advancement undertakings can encourage the organization of COVID-19. The characteristics of individuals and private regions can enhance each other by giving information and cautioning organizations that address the necessities of focal individuals in the food deftly chain (Workie et al. 2020).

2 Digital agriculture courses
Applying progressed advancements can help farmers in accepting work and data-saving practices. Advances that interface farmers to buyers and collaboration organizations can help limit the impact of the pandemic on the nimble chain. Moreover, automated developments will enable us to see even more unquestionably the impact of the pandemic on agricultural creation, work availability, input deftly, and collaborations.

3 Price control
The stronger the information about government procedures and exercises concern the food and agriculture product price control.

4 Develop online market
The internet connections are well developed in the majority of Malaysia's cities; the majority of urban residents can access information online. A public database of contacts and information about farm producers in order to associate farm producers with customers directly will be helpful for the online market, which will offer a feasible solution to delivering farm goods directly to customers.

5 Promoting food crop
A possible strategy would be to look for ways to offer incentives to farmers to grow food crops. Malaysia currently imports about 30% of its food needs per year. Despite substantial increases in the local production of food such as rice, beef, fish, eggs, oils, vegetables, and fruits over the years, our reliance on food imports remains high. This is partly because local food production is still not capable of meeting the demand of the country's growing population. The key explanation for

lower local food production is lower import food prices, which causes farmers to turn to grow cash crops rather than food crops.

6 Seed bank
Establish a seed bank for food crops to ensure the sustainability of genetic germplasm for crop diversification. The seeds' possible genetic diversity will be a valuable advantage for breeders and farmers trying to achieve agricultural resilience. The seed bank's role will be to act as a reserve for us to draw from in order to ensure a steady supply of good starting growing material (Chin, 2020).

7 Green fertilizer
A farmer still might adopt a new agricultural practice even though it might not result in a direct profit. It is possible in reality through some financial initiatives, such as capital subsidies for the maintenance and set-up of green fertilizer, reduction in tax for the green fertilizer adopters, reducing the rate of interest, and complimentary technical for green fertilizer adoption to save costs hence increase yields. These initiatives could secondarily reshape the perceived profitability of farmers and enhance real farm profitability (Adnan & Nordin 2021).

8 Innovation incentives
More resources should be given to support innovation studies and programmes that increase productivity, minimise production losses, and encourage value-adding activities in agriculture and associated non-agriculture projects.

Acknowledgement

The author would like to thank the Universiti Malaya COVID-19 related special research grant (CSRG007-2020SS) for the funding for this research and to all students of AID2009 Agriculture and Environment Session 2020/2021 for their primary data inputs.

Summary

The impact of COVID-19 on Malaysia's agriculture sector are:

- The COVID-19 pandemic has short-term and long-term implications in agriculture sector operation.
- The impact of COVID-19 on the agriculture sector is a chain effect from agriculture production to the food supply.
- COVID-19 impacts are more severe in poor agriculture countries where the agriculture production system is more labour intensive and dependent on imported inputs.

References

Adnan, N., & Nordin, S. M. (2021). How COVID 19 effect Malaysian paddy industry? Adoption of green fertilizer a potential resolution. *Environment, Development and Sustainability* 23, 8089–8129. https://doi.org/10.1007/s10668-020-00978-6

Chin, C. F. (2020). The impact of food supply chain disruptions amidst COVID-19 in Malaysia. *Journal of Agriculture, Food Systems, and Community Development*, 9(4), 161–163. https://doi.org/10.5304/jafscd.2020.094.031

Fair Labor Association. (2020). COVID-19 and migrant agriculture workers in the palm oil sector in Malaysia: recommendations for protecting workers. https://www.fairlabor.org/sites/default/files/protecting-palm-oil-workers-malaysia.pdf.

Kumar, P. S. Singh, A. Pandey, R. K. Singh, P. K. Srivastava, M. Kumar, ..., M. Drews. (2021). Multi-level impacts of the COVID-19 lockdown on agricultural systems in India: The case of Uttar Pradesh. *Agricultural Systems*, 187, 103027, https://doi.org/10.1016/j.agsy.2020.103027

Dina Murad (2020). Beefing up food security. *The Star* Online. https://www.thestar.com.my/news/focus/2020/04/19/beefing-up-food-security.

OECD. (2020). Policy responses to coronavirus (COVID-19) COVID-19 and the food and agriculture sector: Issues and policy responses. 29 April 2020. https://www.oecd.org/coronavirus/policy-responses/covid-19-and-the-food-and-agriculture-sector-issues-and-policy-responses-a23f764b/

Rashidah Abd Rahim. (2020, Nov 8). COVID-19 impacts on poultry egg industry-Association. Bernama. https://www.bernama.com/en/general/news_covid-19.php?id=1898687.

Siche, R. (2020). What is the impact of COVID-19 disease on agriculture?. *Scientia Agropecuaria* 11(1): 3–6.

Supriya S. (2020). Edge Weekly: Cover Story: MCO casts spotlight on 'disconnect' in agribusiness supply chain. The Edge Malaysia Weekly April 24, 2020 17:00 pm +08. This article first appeared in The Edge Malaysia Weekly, on April 13, 2020 to April 19, 2020.

USDA Foreign Agricultural Service Malaysia. (2020). Agriculture sector: This is a best prospect industry sector for this country. Includes a market overview and trade data. Malaysia - Country Commercial Guide. https://www.trade.gov/knowledge-product/malaysia-agricultural-sector.

Workie, E., Mackolil, J., Nyika, J., & Ramadas, S. (2020). Deciphering the impact of COVID-19 pandemic on food security, agriculture, and livelihoods: A review of the evidence from developing countries. *Current Research in Environmental Sustainability*, 2, 100014. https://doi.org/10.1016/j.crsust.2020.100014

Zhang, X. (2020). Chinese livestock farms struggle under COVID-19 restrictions. Research Post of International Food Policy Research Institute. https://www.ifpri.org/blog/chinese-livestock-farmsstruggle-under-COVID-19.

3 The impact of COVID-19 on business resilience in Malaysia

Insights from Kelantan

Noraida Saidi and Normaizatul Akma Saidi

3.1 Introduction

The COVID-19 pandemic, which started in Wuhan, China, at the end of 2019, has had a devastating impact on the business' sustainability worldwide. This is because most countries around the world, including Malaysia, have decided to implement movement control orders (MCO) to prevent the spread of the virus. During the first MCO from March to May 2020, only companies that provide basic necessities were allowed to operate their businesses, while companies from other sectors had to close their operations temporarily for about two months from March to April 2020. In the United States, Yelp.com's Local Economic Impact Report has shown that 97,966 companies have permanently closed their operations due to COVID-19. Whereby, in Malaysia, Social Security Organisation has reported that 2,713 SMEs in Malaysia have closed their operation for a period between March and October 2020 even though 221 of them had received financial aid in terms of the Social Security Organisation's Wage Subsidy Programme (Achariam, 2020). Therefore, COVID-19 has economically affected all businesses around the world, both incorporated entities and small-medium enterprises.

The recent studies regarding the impact of COVID-19 on 3,194 SMEs in China have revealed the different impacts on different categories of industry such as poor logistic problem for primary industry, supply chain management problem for the manufacturing industry, the problem with online services for wholesale and retail trade industry, cashflow pressures for the hospitality industry and short-term pressures were faced by the Chinese's new economy industry (Lu et al., 2021). Another study has revealed some impact of COVID-19 on 1,207 SMEs in Pakistan whereby 96% of the SMEs have to close their business operation due to government-mandated closure, 74% of SMEs have faced a decrease in demand for products and services, 72% of SMEs have a shortage of supplies or inputs,

DOI: 10.4324/9781003182740-3

68% of SMEs have faced difficulty in moving or shipping goods and 13% respondents reported an increase in demand for products or services during MCO (Aftab et al., 2021). The same situation was faced by Malaysian SMEs whereby the 6 of the respondents reported the problems regarding business operation such as operation disruptions, supply chain disruptions, fore sighting the future business direction and the financial problems such as cash flow imbalance, access to stimulus packages and risk of bankruptcy (Che Omar et al., 2020). The previous studies have proven the severity of the impact of COVID-19 on business sustainability, especially for SMEs, due to limited resources.

In addition, previous studies also have discussed the strategies adopted by companies in coping with the impact of COVID-19. For example, Che Omar et al. (2020) have found that SMEs have applied these two survival strategies during MCO, which are financial strategy by minimising the debt, adopting business flexibility strategy and utilising internal strategic resources and marketing strategy by adapting electronic and social media marketing. Besides, innovation strategy has been identified as a source of organisational resilience for small businesses in the manufacturing and service industry (Caballero-Morales, 2021; Thukral, 2021). This review shows that business resilience plays a significant role in determining the ability of the business to cope with business disruptions due to COVID-19.

Based on the above-mentioned arguments, this chapter is intended to study two main research objectives. The first objective is to explore the financial management practices of small and medium enterprises (SMEs) in Kelantan. The second objective is to explore the core competencies of small business owners in Kelantan in shaping the business' resilience to cope with the impact of COVID-19.

3.1.1 Business resilience

In the context of the organisation, following Ates and Bititci (2011), resilience is defined as "the ability to anticipate key opportunities and events from emerging trends, constantly adapting and changing, rapidly bouncing back from disaster and remaining stable in a turbulent environment". In line with this definition, business resilience is seen as the ability of business owners to respond to the changes in the business environment. These abilities are always referred to core competencies, such as operational knowledge and skills, strategic initiatives and talent management (Krishnan, 2020). Besides, Wang et al. (2004) have cited the definition of core competency from Bogner and Thomas, (1994), which refers to an organisation's specific skills and cognitive traits that can lead towards achieving the highest level of customer satisfaction compared to competitors. The following discussed the element of core competencies that are suitable to be exploited in shaping small business' resilience.

Furthermore, Ng et al. (2020) have discussed three aspects of core competencies that affect the company's financial performance, namely transformational leadership, entrepreneurial competence and technical competence. First, transformational leadership refers to the entrepreneurial leadership style that drives a business to transformative change, including inspiring and motivating its employees to work on new ideas to achieve extraordinary performance beyond expectations. Transformational leadership in question is a leader who positively envisions the future scenario of the company and enhances the self-potential of each of its employees to realise the mission and vision of the company together (İşcan et al., 2014). The following section discussed entrepreneurial competence.

In addition, entrepreneurial competence refers to the ability to combine the knowledge, skills and collective resources of the company that will improve the position of the company and its products as well as attract customers to buy with the right marketing methods (Wang et al., 2004). Then, Mitchelmore and Rowley (2010) have discussed entrepreneurial competence in the context of SMEs, which depends on the demographic background of an entrepreneur, psychological and behavioural characteristics, as well as their technical skills and knowledge that can influence the success of an SME. The literature review also found three different mechanisms by which entrepreneurial competence can influence performance. First, more efficient entrepreneurs take advantage of every available business opportunity. Second, efficient management related to business strategy, more efficient entrepreneurs can formulate superior strategies that suit their business. Thus, these entrepreneurial competencies are important for all SMEs in giving quick responses to the impact of COVID-19.

Lastly, technical competence refers to the expertise of business owners in technical or functional areas (Chandler & Jensen, 1992). This is because every SME entrepreneur usually has their own field of expertise. For example, livestock farm operators have in-depth technical knowledge of plantations. This technical knowledge will help the entrepreneur to make the right decision compared to entrepreneurs who do not have technical competence in the ventured businesses. Previous studies have also used different terminology to assess technical competencies, i.e., operational efficiency, that emphasises the ability of organisations to use their buckets to support supply chain capabilities (Ngai et al., 2011). Thus, the technical expertise of business owners plays a significant role to ensure that small business owners could utilise their expertise to cope with the impact of COVID-19.

Previous studies have reported that one of the impacts of COVID-19 was the financial problem as a result of disruption of business operations due to MCO (Che Omar et al., 2020; Klein & Todesco, 2021). Thus, the ability of the small business owners to manage their financial management practices could influence business' survival during MCO. This is because companies with poor financial management practices will have a negative impact on company's profits (Wadesango et al., 2019). Financial management practices refer to the strategies applied by companies in managing the fund to achieve the business' objectives and to maximise the shareholder's wealth (Musah et al., 2018). These practices include working capital management (Musah et al., 2018; Al Breiki & Nobanee, 2019; Sa'eed et al., 2020), capital structure management, accounting information system, fixed assets management (Musah et al., 2018; Sa'eed et al., 2020), capital budgeting technique (Musah et al., 2018; Al Breiki & Nobanee, 2019) and the cost of capital (Al Breiki & Nobanee, 2019). Therefore, identifying the financial management practices adopted by SMEs would be useful in evaluating the current state of their financial management practice for further improvement.

3.1.2 Conceptual framework

The conceptual framework as depicted in Figure 3.1 demonstrates the objectives of this study to explore the business resilience of SMEs in Malaysia by exploiting the core competencies of the business owners and their experience in managing financial management practices. For example, efficient financial management practices can be achieved through well-maintained working capital and cash flow management. The business owners need to optimise the amount of working capital to avoid the additional cost of acquiring idle assets due to excess of working capital. Besides, too little amount of working capital also could lead to solvency problems (Ojera, 2018; Sa'eed et al., 2020). During MCO, the efficient management of working capital which covers both aspects of current assets and current liabilities, including trade credit and sales policies, plays a vital role in minimising the risk of financial difficulties due to temporary disclosure of business operations. Thus, the ability of the business to do efficient financial management practices in surviving with the financial problems due to COVID-19 could develop their business resilience and sustainability.

Furthermore, the business resilience could be achieved by exploiting the business' core competencies. Firstly, the leaders which are the business owners play a significant role for any business transformation action. They would positively envision the future scenario of the company, enhances the self-potential of each of its employees to realise the

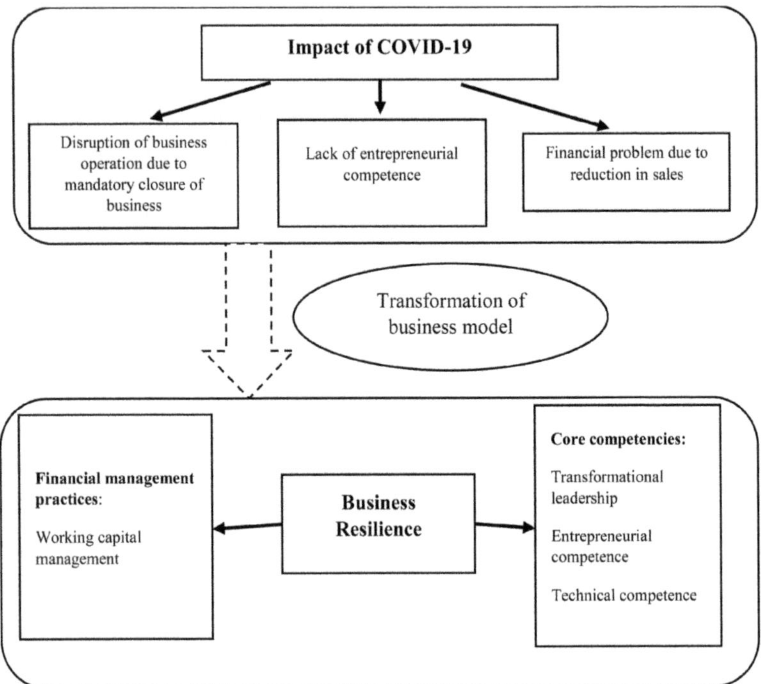

Figure 3.1 Conceptual framework of SME's business resilience during COVID-19

mission and vision of the company together (İşcan et al., 2014) and able to foster an innovative work ethic among employees (Amankwaa et al., 2019). Secondly, the business transformation plan cannot be achieved without right entrepreneurial knowledge and skills. Abd Ghani and Darawi (2012) have revealed that business management skills play an important role for business success, especially during MCO. They need to seize every business opportunity around them and explore new business opportunities that have not been explored by others to be more competitive. In addition, Wang et al. (2004) have evaluated entrepreneurial competence from the marketing aspect to company performance. This is because a company that wisely combines the knowledge, skills and collective resources of the company will improve the position of the company and its products as well as attract customers to buy with the right marketing methods. Lastly, the technical competence of business owners shall influence the success of business transformation during MCO. These technical competencies would boost the ability of business owners to innovate their products and services to develop their business resilience due to COVID-19.

3.2 Method

3.2.1 Design

A qualitative approach was employed in this study to explore the impact of COVID-19 on financial management practices and core competencies of SME owners in Kelantan. Guest et al. (2014) have quoted the definition of qualitative research by Nkwi et al. (2001) "Qualitative research involves any research that uses data that do not indicate ordinal values". This definition fits this study as the data generated from qualitative inquiry are non-numeric and less structured in the form of text because the data collection process itself offers more flexibility and inductive in nature (Guest et al., 2014). The text has been used as a proxy of the experience of participants under inquiry in order to capture their perceptions, feelings, knowledge and behaviours regarding the impact of COVID-19 on their business resilience.

This study has employed an open-ended online survey which was designed through Google form to collect data from participants via online platforms like Facebook Messenger, WhatsApp Message and email. This open-ended online survey was used as it is practical for both participants and researchers with resources and time constraints (Braun et al., 2020). It has some advantageous features like participants can answer the survey questions at any time at their own places, which could reduce the risk of researcher's personal health safety such as getting infected by the COVID-19 virus (Grogan et al., 2018; Braun et al., 2020). Next, Braun et al. (2020) has further argued that an online survey shall provide a wide-angle lens on the topic of interest, which is to capture the perspective of SME owners regarding their practices of financial management and core competencies that influencing their resilience which leads to their business survival during COVID-19 pandemic. Braun et al. (2020) further highlighted that online qualitative surveys datasets could achieve richness and in-depth information when they were viewed as whole, even if some responses might provide brief information. Despite all the above advantages, this method has some weaknesses, such as the researchers are not able to do the direct observation of the participants to capture their expression of feelings and real condition of the affected businesses due to COVID-19 (Patton, 2002).

3.2.2 Participants

The research being exploratory in nature, it was decided to conduct the research using qualitative research techniques. The purposeful sampling technique was adopted to select only information-rich cases which can provide an insight about the phenomenon under inquiry which is the impact of COVID-19 on the business' resilience in Kelantan from the perspective of financial management practices and core competencies (Patton, 2002; Obazee, 2019). As this study used information-rich cases with small sample size, the findings of this study cannot be generalised to the whole population of SMEs in Kelantan and other states in Malaysia.

The inclusion criteria as research participants were that SMEs owners must have gone through the temporary closure of business operations due to movement control order for a period between March 2020 and May 2020. The second criteria were all participants must understand the Malay language as the open-ended online survey was in Malay. The exclusion criteria were those SME owners in the industries in need who can operate their business during MCO and those who did not understand the Malay language. The authors enlisted SMEs known to the authors, who were contacted via Facebook Messenger and WhatsApp with a brief description of the objectives of the study for subsequent consent before the open-ended online survey was sent to the participants. This study applied the sample size suggested by Braun et al., (2020) for qualitative online surveys, which start from the range of 20–49 samples for lower end sample size. This sample size has been applied by previous studies for qualitative online surveys (Grogan et al., 2018; Braun et al., 2020). However, this study manages to collect only 11 respondents from 11 SMEs owners throughout Kelantan State, which have been gathered for a period of two months in January and February 2021 through online platforms like Facebook Messenger and WhatsApp.

Based on Table 3.1 of the demographic profile, all of the participants meet the definition of SMEs in Malaysia under small categories (2 samples) and micro categories (9 samples) based on the annual sales volume and number of full-time employees. Ten of the sample participants are from service and other sectors, and only one sample participant is from the manufacturing sector. Majority of the sample participants (5) are new businesses with less than five years' experience. Two of them have been doing business for more than 5 years and three of them are considered mature in the business industry with more than 10 years of experience in business. All of these sample participants have faced problems in their business operations due to COVID-19.

3.2.3 Materials

The questions for the online survey were constructed based on the previous literature to explore the impact of new phenomenon, which is COVID-19, on the business resilience of SME owners in Kelantan in terms of financial

Table 3.1 Demographic profile of the firm owned by the participant

Participant	*Business location*	*Business sector*	*Yearly sales*	*Firm age*	*Size (number of employees)*
A	Kota Bharu	Other sectors	Between RM300,000 and RM3 million	6–10 years	5–29
B	Pasir Puteh	Service	Below RM300,000	1–5 years	0–4
C	Kota Bharu	Service	Below RM300,000	11–15 years	0–4
D	Kota Bharu	Service	Between RM300,000 and RM3 million	6–10 years	5–29
E	Pasir Puteh	Other sectors	Below RM300,000	1–5 years	0–4
F	Kota Bharu	Service	Below RM300,000	16 years and above	0–4
G	Kota Bharu	Service	Below RM300,000	1–5 years	0–4
H	Kota Bharu	Service	Below RM300,000	1–5 years	0–4
I	Kota Bharu	Other sectors	Below RM300,000	16 years and above	0–4
J	Bachok	Service	Below RM300,000	1–5 years	0–4
K	Tanah Merah	Manufacturing	Below RM300,000	16 years and above	0–4

management practices and core competencies of SME owners. Questions comprise three parts whereby part A seeks for demographic and general information regarding the problems faced by SME owners during movement control order. Part B of the survey seeks to gauge the core competencies possessed by SME owners in Kelantan when handling the issues faced due to COVID-19. Lastly, Part C of the survey seeks to explore the financial management practices applied by SME owners in Kelantan that could shape their business resilience during movement control order.

3.2.4 Procedure

The data collection process was done through an online platform where a link to the Google form was sent to participants through Facebook Messenger, WhatsApp or email. The data collection started with an ethical statement whereby the participants were informed about the purpose of the survey, and their consent to take part in the survey was considered granted when they clicked "next" in the survey form. The participants also were provided with the contact number and email address of the researcher in the event of further inquiries to answer the survey question.

3.2.5 Data analysis

All participants have responded to all questions provided in the survey with a combination of brief and in-depth answers. The data from an online open-ended survey was extracted in the form of an excel sheet. Afterwards, all the answers in the excel sheet were translated manually into the English language. Thematic content analysis was used to analyse the data as this is the prominent data analysis used in qualitative research (Guest et al., 2014; Grogan et al., 2018; Braun et al., 2020; Manyati & Mutsau, 2021). Thematic analysis is a method for identifying, analysing, organising, describing, and reporting themes found within a data set (Braun & Clarke, 2006 as cited in Nowell et al., 2017). This study has followed strategies presented by Nowell et al. (2017) in conducting thematic analysis to achieve trustworthiness of results whereby it involved six phases as depicted in Table 3.2.

Table 3.2 Phase of thematic analysis for core competencies and financial management practices among SME owners in Kelantan

Phase of thematic analysis	*Means of establishing trustworthiness*
Phase 1: Familiarising yourself with the data	• Prolong engagement with the data • Store raw data in well-organised archives
Phase 2: Generating Initial Codes	• Peer debriefing • Researcher triangulation
Phase 3: Searching for Themes	• Researcher triangulation • Diagramming to make sense of theme connections
Phase 4: Reviewing Themes	• Researcher triangulation • Themes and sub-themes vetted by team members
Phase 5: Defining and Naming Themes	• Researcher triangulation • Peer debriefing • Peer consensus on themes
Phase 6: Producing the Report	• Member checking • Peer debriefing

3.3 Findings

The inductive approach has been used to analyse the data. The thematic analysis has revealed **three themes** (see Sections 3.3.1 to 3.3.3) on how the SME owners in Kelantan dealt with the business challenges faced during the movement control order due to COVID-19. The core competencies and financial management practices were discussed in detail in the following themes.

3.3.1 Transformation of business management

3.3.1.1 Utilisation of the internet of thing in managing business operation

The internet has become one of the most important elements in the business operations of SME owners during the movement control order due to COVID-19. Three of the respondents have fully utilised the benefits of the internet by integrating the online business in their business operation during MCO as shown below. This is because most SME owners could not operate their physical business during MCO. By doing online business, they can reach the customers beyond their normal course of business since most of the potential customers in Malaysia have a smartphone as their communication tool.

> "We utilize online business mode over counter sales" – Respondent A
> "Try online business initiative"- Respondent C
> "Yes, now move to online business"- Respondent F

In addition, the marketing of products or services also can be done online. Six of the respondents have used the online platform including social media like Facebook, Instagram and Twitter to promote their products or services during MCO. SME owners also need to engage in heavy and creative promotion during MCO to attract customers buying their products or services. This is because most of the SME owners have experienced a reduction in sales revenue (up to 80%) due to the closure of their business operation at the beginning of MCO.

> "Focus on online business"—Respondent A
> "Through social media"—Respondent C
> "Online"—Respondent E
> "Increase online marketing…"—Respondent F
> "Through online platform…"—Respondent J
> "Use or prepare soft sell & hard sell marketing in social media platforms like Instagram, Facebook & Twitter"—Respondent K

However, every transformation in the business operation could not be derived without a transformational leader. SME owners, as the leaders, have taken the initiatives to do online business in order to achieve the business objectives. This is supported by previous studies who found that leaders with a positive attitude (Madanchian & Taherdoost, 2019), innovative envision (Amankwaa et al., 2019), which enhance the self-potential of employees (İşcan et al., 2014) could give positive influence on the financial performance of SMEs.

3.3.1.2 Venture into new business opportunities

Furthermore, the sub-theme for the transformation of business management is done when two of the SME owners in Kelantan ventured into new business opportunities in order to continue their business operation during MCO. Besides, some of the SME owners also have changed the standard of operation by adding additional services to the customers, such as providing delivery services in order to increase the sales. This is supported by previous studies who found that business management skills could benefit the business owners to explore new business opportunities (Abd Ghani & Darawi, 2012) and innovative products (Ng et al., 2020) to remain competitive in the industry.

> "Due to the worsening COVID-19 pandemic, I decided to try a new business" – Respondent B
>
> "Try another business for side income" – Respondent H

3.3.2 Technical expertise of core competencies

The results of the survey revealed that technical expertise of SME owners has helped them in facing the difficulties during MCO. One of the SME owners has used the marketing knowledge to attract more customers during MCO, whereby another respondent used the technical skills in generating additional income during MCO. This is supported by Wijaya and Irianto (2018) who found that technical skills of managers which are unique, irreplaceable, rare and limited could give a positive impact on companies' performance. The following responses have described that the element of technical core competencies of SME owners plays an important role in an organisation during challenging period:

> "This marketing knowledge helps me to attract customers with my services" – Respondent B
>
> "Assist in terms of maintenance cost savings" – Respondent D

"I can offer special menus and change menus to attract customers" – Respondent G

"With computer repair expertise, a lot of demand because many use computers during MCO" – Respondent K

"It can help me by applying the right and efficient ways in managing a business. In terms of choosing the right type of goods, managing capital and also earning a suitable profit and not loss" – Respondent L

3.3.3 *Effective financial management practices*

3.3.3.1 *Financial management*

Financial management is vital to the overall health of the business. The results demonstrated that the majority of the business owners had established cash flow control and monitoring during difficult times, especially during MCO. The majority of the respondents implemented the cash flow control by allowing only cash sales and paying off debts regularly. Besides that, the other respondent minimised the amount invested in stock in order to maintain adequate amounts of cash for business survival. This is consistent with previous studies that stated the reduction in investment in working capital by reducing the amount of inventory and account receivable would lead to an increase in the firm's performance (Afrifa & Tingbani, 2018).

"Cash sales and cash management are important by paying off debts regularly" – Respondent A

"Separating capital and profits" – Respondent B

"Save every day for your own salary and have to save for premise rental payment. In order not to be burdened when it comes time to rent payment" – Respondent G

"Stop all restaurant operations, relax all employees, save on daily expenses in order to survive MCO" – Respondent I

"Never use the profits and capital earned at will. Make the right capital decision especially in term of stock purchase" – Respondent K

3.3.3.2 *Cash flow management*

A neat and sustainable financial record is crucial to the business. Based on the survey, most of the respondents recorded their transaction. All the transactions involved are recorded accordingly via various methods of recording, i.e., cloud accounting, book and excel worksheet. Then, the recorded transactions can be used as a reference for the firm's financial condition. Therefore, the managers or owners who possessed a higher level of financial knowledge tend to record all the detailed financial records (Harianti et al., 2021).

> "Money in and out reports are updated daily on the company's financial group Whatsapp. There is a threshold value for money coming in, if it is less than that amount, then the sales division needs to double the effort"—Respondent A
>
> "Need to manage cash flow wisely with the current situation that does not know when all this will end. The spa sector is very challenging business because all spa has to close immediately"—Respondent C
>
> "Record all transactions"—Respondent D
>
> "Record in the book, daily sales revenue"—Respondent G
>
> "Spend with caution and only spend on basic necessities"—Respondent I
>
> "Use Cloud accounting to record daily sales"—Respondent J
>
> "Record in laptop and excel"—Respondent K

3.3.3.3 Problems related to working capital management

Working capital management is vital for the smooth running of the business operation. Nevertheless, the dynamic nature of the working capital makes it challenging for the managers or owners to maintain the required level of working capital. There are three respondents who revealed that they are having problems with the debtors due to the MCO. Therefore, this debtor's problem will affect their firm's profitability in the long run. Previous research highlights that failure to keep up the required level of working capital would affect a firm's profitability (Ahangar, 2021; Sawarni et al., 2021).

> "Since MCO there has been a problem with debtors" – Respondent C
>
> "Yes. The debtor cannot pay the amount due. Thus, I cannot replace stock" – Respondent H

3.4 Conclusion

The key findings of this study revealed that the sustainability of small and medium enterprises in emerging countries during the world health crisis would depend on the core competencies possessed by SME owners or managers of SME businesses. Table 3.3 summarises the key findings of this research.

Table 3.3 Summary of core competencies and financial management practices among SME owners in Kelantan

No.	*Theme*	*Sub-theme*
1	Transformation of Business Management	i Utilisation of internet of thing in managing business operation ii Venture into new business opportunities
2	Technical expertise of core competencies	–
3	Effective Financial management practices	i Financial management ii Cash flow management iii Problems related to working capital management

Transformational leadership of SME owners or managers is the ability to provide positive encouragement to employees through positive attitudes and innovative ideas to deal with the new norm in managing business (online business) during movement control order due to COVID-19. Besides, entrepreneurial and technical competence also plays a vital role in accelerating the adaptation of SME owners to the new business model in their business operation during MCO. In the aspect of financial management practices, SME owners' main concern is the working capital management including efficient management of cash to enable the business going concern. Viewed in the context of current challenges that SMEs face, it is worthwhile to invest resources in enhancing the current core competencies to remain viable in the current and future challenges. For the policymakers, the findings of this study suggest that Malaysian government must empower the core competencies, including leadership and entrepreneurial skills for SME business, especially for micro and small categories of SMEs.

Since this is an exploratory study with a limited number of participants, an empirical study examining the influence of core competencies and financial management practices on firm performance might be relevant to provide better insights into current issues faced by SMEs and gain better understanding on the development, survival and growth of SMEs. This research only considers from the perspective of SMEs in Kelantan as a sample size. Therefore, it is recommended for future research to enlarge the sample size that includes other states of the country in order to enable comparison of the performance of SMEs in Malaysia. Lastly, future research can also reconsider this research by extending the analysis to include both qualitative and quantitative surveys for better understanding.

Summary

- Transformational leadership of SME owners or managers is the ability to provide positive encouragement to employees.
- The entrepreneurial and technical competence plays a vital role in accelerating the adaptation of SME owners to the new business model.
- In the aspect of financial management practices, the working capital management, including efficient management of cash, becomes the main concern of the SME owners to enable the business going concerned.

References

Abd Ghani, M. A., & Darawi, Z. (2012). Transformasi dan prestasi perniagaan usahawan Melayu perusahaan kecil dan sederhana (PKS) di Johor Bahru. *Prosiding Persidangan Kebangsaan Ekonomi Malaysia Ke VII*, 697.

Achariam, T. (2020, November 18). Covid-19: 2,713 SMEs closed down between March and October 2020. The Edge Markets: Malaysia Edition. https://www.theedgemarkets.com/article/covid19-2713-smes-closed-down-between-march-and-oct-2020

Ahangar, N. (2021). Is the relationship between working capital management and firm profitability non-linear in Indian SMEs? *Small Enterprise Research*, 28(1), 23–35. https://doi.org/10.1080/13215906.2021.18726

Afrifa, G., & Tingbani, I. (2018). Working capital management, cash flow and SMEs' performance. *International Journal of Banking Accounting and Finance*, *9*(1), 19–43.

Aftab, R., Naveed, M., & Hanif, S. (2021). An analysis of Covid-19 implications for SMEs in Pakistan. *Journal of Chinese Economic and Foreign Trade Studies, 14*(1), 74–88. https://doi.org/10.1108/JCEFTS-08-2020-0054

Al Breiki, M., & Nobanee, H. (2019). The role of financial management in promoting sustainable business practices and development. *SSRN Electronic Journal.* https://doi.org/10.2139/ssrn.3472404

Amankwaa, A., Gyensare, M. A., & Susomrith, P. (2019). Transformational leadership with innovative behaviour: examining multiple mediating paths with PLS-SEM. *Leadership and Organization Development Journal*, *40*(4), 402–420. https://doi.org/10.1108/LODJ-10-2018-0358

Ates, A., & Bititci, U. (2011). Change process: a key enabler for building resilient SMEs. *International Journal of Production Research*, *49*(18), 5601–5618. https://doi.org/10.1080/00207543.2011.563825

Bogner, W. C., & Thomas, H. (1994). Core competencies and competitive advantage: A model and illustrative evidence from the pharmaceutical industry. In G. Hamel and A. Heene (Eds.), *Competence Based Competition* (pp. 111–144). Chichester, New York: Wiley.

Braun, V., & Clarke, V. (2006). Using thematic analysis in psychology. *Qualitative Research in Psychology*, *3*(2), 77–101. https://doi.org/10.1191/1478088706qp063oa

Braun, V., Clarke, V., Boulton, E., Davey, L., & McEvoy, C. (2020). The online survey as a qualitative research tool. *International Journal of Social Research Methodology*, 1–14. https://doi.org/10.1080/13645579.2020.1805550

Caballero-Morales, S. O. (2021). Innovation as recovery strategy for SMEs in emerging economies during the COVID-19 pandemic. *Research in International Business and Finance, 57,* 101396. https://doi.org/10.1016/j.ribaf.2021.101396

Chandler, G. N., & Jansen, E. (1992). The founder's self-assessed competence and venture performance. *Journal of Business Venturing, 7,* 223–236.

Che Omar, A. R., Ishak, S., & Jusoh, M. A. (2020). The impact of Covid-19 Movement Control Order on SMEs' businesses and survival strategies. *Malaysian Journal of Society and Space, 16*(2), 139–150. https://doi.org/10.17576/geo-2020-1602-11

Grogan, S., Turley, E., & Cole, J. (2018). "So many women suffer in silence": a thematic analysis of women's written accounts of coping with endometriosis. *Psychology and Health, 33*(11), 1364–1378. https://doi.org/https://doi.org/10.1080/08870446.2018.1496252

Guest, G., MacQueen, K., & Namey, E. (2014). Introduction to applied thematic analysis. *Applied Thematic Analysis,* 3–20. https://doi.org/10.4135/9781483384436.n1

Harianti, A., Malinda, M., Tjandra, M., & Kambuno, D. (2021). Descriptive analysis of financial literacy SMEs in Bandung. *International Journal of Trade, Economics and Finance, 12*(1), 9–15. https://doi.org/10.18178/ijtef.2021.12.1.686

İşcan, Ö. F., Ersarı, G., & Naktiyok, A. (2014). Effect of leadership style on perceived organizational performance and innovation: the role of transformational leadership beyond the impact of transactional leadership – an application among Turkish SME's. *Procedia – Social and Behavioral Sciences, 150,* 881–889. https://doi.org/10.1016/j.sbspro.2014.09.097

Klein, V. B., & Todesco, J. L. (2021). COVID-19 crisis and SMEs responses: The role of digital transformation. *Knowledge and Process Management, August 2020,* 1–17. https://doi.org/10.1002/kpm.1660

Krishnan, D. (2020). A hierarchical model to enhance financial and strategic performance of an oil and gas company in Malaysia. *International Journal of Energy Sector Management, 14*(2), 482–503. https://doi.org/10.1108/IJESM-01-2019-0001

Lu, L., Peng, J., Wu, J., & Lu, Y. (2021). Perceived impact of the Covid-19 crisis on SMEs in different industry sectors: Evidence from Sichuan, China. *International Journal of Disaster Risk Reduction, 55*(24). https://doi.org/10.1016/j.ijdrr.2021.102085

Madanchian, M., & Taherdoost, H. (2019). Assessment of leadership effectiveness dimensions in small medium enterprises (SMEs). *Procedia Manufacturing, 32,* 1035–1042. https://doi.org/10.1016/j.promfg.2019.02.318

Manyati, T. K., & Mutsau, M. (2021). Leveraging green skills in response to the COVID-19 crisis: a case study of small and medium enterprises in Harare, Zimbabwe. *Journal of Entrepreneurship in Emerging Economies.* https://doi.org/10.1108/JEEE-07-2020-0236

Mitchelmore, S., & Rowley, J. (2010). Entrepreneurial competencies: A literature review and development agenda. *International Journal of Entrepreneurial Behaviour & Research, 16*(2), 92–111. https://doi.org/10.1108/13552551011026995

Musah, A., Gakpetor, E. D., & Pomaa, P. (2018). Financial management practices, firm growth and profitability of small and medium scale enterprises (SMEs). *Information Management and Business Review*, *10*(3), 25–37.

Ng, H. S., Kee, D. M. H., Ramayah, T., Hefferon, K., & Gil-rodriguez, E. (2020). Examining the mediating role of innovativeness in the link between core competencies and SME performance. *Journal of Small Business and Enterprise Development*, *27*(1), 103–129. https://doi.org/10.1108/JSBED-12-2018-0379

Nkwi, P., Nyamongo, I., & Ryan, G. (2001). *Field research into socio-cultural issues: Methodological guidelines*. Yaounde, Cameroon: International Center for Applied Social Sciences, Research, and Training/UNFPA.

Nowell, L. S., Norris, J. M., White, D. E., & Moules, N. J. (2017). Thematic analysis: striving to meet the trustworthiness criteria. *International Journal of Qualitative Methods*, *16*(1), 1–13. https://doi.org/10.1177/1609406917733847

Obazee, A. T. (2019). *Exploring Financial Management Practices of Small and Medium-Sized Enterprises in Nigeria*. Walden University.

Ojera, P. (2018). Indigenous financial management practices in Africa: A guide for educators and practitioners. *Advanced Series in Management*, *20*, 71–96. https://doi.org/10.1108/S1877-636120180000020005

Patton, M. Q. (2002). Two decades of developments in qualitative inquiry: a personal, experiential perspective. *Qualitative Social Work*, *1*(3), 261–283. https://doi.org/10.1177/1473325002001003636

Sa'eed, A., Gambo, N., Ibrahim Inuwa, I., & Musonda, I. (2020). Effects of financial management practices on technical performance of building contractors in northeast Nigeria. *Journal of Financial Management of Property and Construction*, *25*(2), 201–223. https://doi.org/10.1108/JFMPC-07-2019-0064

Sawarni, K. S., Narayanasamy, S., & Ayyalusamy, K. (2021). Working capital management, firm performance and nature of business: An empirical evidence from India. *International Journal of Productivity and Performance Management*, *70*(1), 179–200. https://doi.org/10.1108/IJPPM-10-2019-0468.

Thukral, E. (2021). COVID-19: Small and medium enterprises challenges and responses with creativity, innovation, and entrepreneurship. *Strategic Change*, *30*(2), 153–158. https://doi.org/10.1002/jsc.2399

Wadesango, N., Tinarwo, N., Sitcha, L., & Machingambi, S. (2019). The impact of cash flow management on the profitability and sustainability of small to medium sized enterprises. *International Journal of Entrepreneurship*, *23*(2), 1–19.

Wang, Y., Lo, H., & Yang, Y. (2004). The constituents of core competencies and firm performance: evidence from high-technology firms in china. *Journal of Engineering and Technology Management*, *21*, 249–280. https://doi.org/10.1016/j.jengtecman.2004.09.001

Wijaya, E. R., & Irianto, D. (2018). Analysis influence of managerial competence, technical competence, and strategic competence on firm performance in electrical engineering company in Bandung. *IOP Conference Series: Materials Science and Engineering*, *319*(1), 0–8. https://doi.org/10.1088/1757-899X/319/1/012081

4 The impact of COVID-19 on corporate social responsibility in Malaysia

Insights from case studies

Nabila Huda Ibrahim

4.1 Introduction

The novel coronavirus COVID-19 has been declared as a pandemic by The World Health Organization (WHO) on 11 March, as the number of cases has reached over 118,000 cases of coronavirus infection in over 110 countries and territories around the world and the sustained risk of further global spread (Ducharme, 2020). As of 11 February 2021, the number of global confirmed cases is 107,807,456, and global deaths are 2,369,471 (Johns Hopkins Coronavirus Resource Center, 2021). Malaysia was well-prepared in facing the COVID-19 after the release of information from Wuhan Municipal of Health Commission on 31 December 2019 about unknown pneumonia and confirmed the very first case on 24 January 2020. As the number of cases was continuously rising, the government of Malaysia imposed the Movement Control Order (MCO) on 18 March 2020 (Tang, 2020). The government efforts on enforcement of MCO, Enhanced MCO, Conditional MCO, and Recovery MCO have been fruitful after Malaysia reported zero COVID-19 cases on 1 July 2020 (Tee, 2020).

The enforcement of MCO has changed the economic landscape of Malaysia. The consumer spending has been reduced, and unemployment rates jumped from 5.0% to 5.3% in April and May 2020. Concurrently, export, import, and trade volumes in April and May have deteriorated and led to a trade deficit of RM3.5 billion in April, which is the first monthly deficit recorded in over 22 years. The economic impacts are expected to be dire with immediate loss of economic activities and possible projections of long-term impact (Zhang et al., 2020).

The unprecedented impact of COVID-19 on the global economy led the government all over the world to establish economic aid packages to ease the pressure (He and Harris, 2020). The role of corporate social responsibility (CSR) has been demanded in mitigating the domino effect

DOI: 10.4324/9781003182740-4

of COVID-19 into the under-performing economy to address the needs of the needy in Malaysia, especially in terms of financial support, safety equipment, and basic necessities. The groups of people who require the aid during COVID-19 are B40 and M40 groups, frontliners in the health sector, frontliners in the security sector, and students (Radzi et al., 2020). The attention to CSR considerations in governments and market participants has been increased due to the pandemic to recover social and environmental loss (Bae et al., 2021).

The framework of CSR can be considered to be derived from the Triple Bottom Line (TBL) theory founded by John Elkington that aims at sustainability. The framework incorporates economic, social, and environmental dimensions of performance. The economic dimension focuses on how organisations achieve continuous profit for the long term. Social dimension describes the importance of business to pay attention to its social affairs at the same par with their financial affairs. It is compulsory for the shareholders to make decisions that satisfy social needs for long-term business stability. Environmental dimension highlights the importance of the organisations to respect the environment to sustain our quality of life for the future generation. To obtain sustainable results, many corporations, both profit and non-profit oriented, have adopted TBL to perform CSR projects (Brin and Nehme, 2019). CSR involves voluntary actions taken by companies that can bring potential effects in terms of corporate costs and social benefits (Gatti et al., 2019).

In this competitive edge of time, the significance of CSR is undeniable as it is closely linked to corporate citizenship and willingness to fulfil its social responsibility. Fulfilling the customers' expectations to work on behalf of society and the environment through CSR will lead a greater long-term advantage. CSR practices improve corporate profitability, image, reputation, and increase consumers' preferences (Kim et al., 2020). CSR initiatives usually encourage improvement and sustain long-term corporate financial performance. However, it is still controversial for the firm to decide whether or not to invest during such a critical time. This is because CSR activities often incur a substantial amount of cost that might undermine the financial well-being while taking off social well-being, which may lead to the company being undervalued in capital markets (Qiu et al., 2021).

During the critical time of COVID-19, the expectations of society for organisation to be socially responsible are tremendous. Since the outbreak, many researchers have addressed the importance of CSR in mitigating the impacts of COVID-19 in various perspectives and areas. The practice of CSR brings potential benefits to organisational sustainability. Ding et al. (2020) found that the impact of the pandemic-induced in stock prices was milder to the organization, which contributed to CSR activities. In terms of human capital, the organisational resilience, including the response of COVID-19 and practice of CSR in hospitality business affect perceived job security of senior managers which influenced their commitment (Filimonau et al., 2020). Employee satisfaction with the corporate COVID-19 responses has positively impacted on employee self-efficacy, hope, resilience and optimism (Mao et al. 2020).

Since the outbreak of the pandemic, many organisations in Malaysia have offered their CSR, which benefits their stakeholders, especially on social contributions. From the perspective of stakeholder theory, this study focuses (i) to analyse the implementation of CSR for the pandemic of COVID-19 and (ii) to what extent it helps in addressing the dilemma of the Malaysian needy. The stakeholder theory refers to the obligations of the managers of the firms to some group of stakeholders (Freeman, 2015). The dimensions of stakeholder of Coronavirus related CSR includes employees, customers, community, shareholders, and the environment (Marom and Lussier, 2020). This study will look into how successful the companies in Malaysia cater to the needs of their stakeholders in combating the impacts of COVID-19 in society.

4.2 Research methodology

This study is a qualitative content analysis that involves secondary data analysis, including annual reports of companies listed under Kuala Lumpur Stock Exchange (KLSE) (Malaysiastock.biz, 2021), newspaper coverage, companies' websites on CSR activities. The reason for employing qualitative content analysis is because it is an autonomous method that can be used to various levels of abstraction and interpretation (Graneheim et al., 2017). The significance of this method is trustworthiness, especially from the raw data without a theory-based categorisation matrix (Elo et al., 2014).

The data collection is divided into two categories, which are (1) CSR in KLSE companies and (2) General companies CSR activities. The data collection is divided into two categories because the data collection was done in early 2021, and many companies have yet to release their Annual Report for the year 2020.

4.2.1 The CSR in KLSE companies

The company listed in KLSE is based on three market choices, namely Main Market, ACE Market and LEAP Market. All these choices have different criteria on quantitative, qualitative, additional criteria for foreign companies and key listing criteria (Bursa Malaysia, 2021). A total of 122 of the latest annual reports from companies listed under KLSE from 30 October 2020 until 29 January 2021 were reviewed, and only information related to CSR on COVID-19 were extracted. Out of 122, only 27 companies reported their CSR activities on COVID-19. The data focuses on the (i) core business, (ii) supports, and (iii) target respondents.

4.2.2 General companies CSR activities

To explore more CSR activities generally, newspaper coverage, companies' websites on CSR activities were accessed. Many companies have contributed to CSR effort on COVID-19 regardless of small or big companies. However, only significant CSR contributions will be selected in this study. The data focuses on the (i) core business, (ii) supports, and (iii) target respondents.

4.3 Findings

Tables 4.1 and 4.2 show the CSR activities done by companies listed in KLSE and other companies, respectively. The findings show that the companies from various backgrounds of core business ranging from manufacturing, services, foods and beverages, and others have contributed to CSR activities related to COVID-19. The target respondents of the CSR activities are frontliners, public health, employees, customers, and the community. The findings of the study are categorised into four types of CSR activities, namely (i) safety and health protections, (ii) customer relationships, (iii) community and social engagement, and (iv) employees' volunteerism. These categories offer different insights on how CSR has been implemented during COVID-19.

4.3.1 Safety and health protections

The findings revealed that most of the companies had spent their money to supply the safety protection equipment, especially to the frontliners, public health, the community, and the employees. The findings supported by Manuel and Herron (2020) for lower-income groups and service sector workers who face greater infection risk, the aid should not just be financial but must also include masks, disinfectants, and other supplies. For the frontliners, the support of the basic necessities and foods were provided to them during this critical time. Public health concerns have been taken care of by the companies that provide the medical supplies, ventilators, personal protective equipment, customised plastic films for wards partition

Table 4.1 The CSR contributions from the companies listed in KLSE

No.	*Company*	*Core business*	*Supports*	*Target respondents*
1	AHB Group (AHB Group, 2020)	Interior Design (Artwright)	Donated daily necessities to the underprivileged group in the residential area of Gombak, Selangor, in collaboration with UMNO Gombak Branch	1 Local community
2	MKH *Berhad* (MKH *Berhad*, 2020)	i Property Development and Constructions ii Plantations iii Property Investments iv Building Materials and Trading	1 More than 100,000 pieces of face masks were donated to the Provincial Government of Kutai Kartanegara and communities near a plantation in East Kalimantan, Indonesia 2 The same essentials were also donated to education institutions, police stations and hospitals in Kajang during MCO and CMCO 3 Invited doctors to conduct swab tests for all employees at the headquarters as a pre-cautionary measure against COVID-19 4 Total amount for overall CSR including related COVID-19 is RM1.7 million	1 Frontliners 2 Under privileged 3 Employees
3	XOX *Berhad* (XOX *Berhad*, 2020)	Telecommunications	1 Donated to various charitable organisations and participated in the internship Program from time to time 2 During MCO: Free 1GB per day community offered to subscribers to support them to keep connected	1 Community/ Customer 2 Needy

(*Continued*)

Table 4.1 (*Continued*)

No.	*Company*	*Core business*	*Supports*	*Target respondents*
4	AEMULUS Holdings *Berhad* (AEMULUS Holdings *Berhad*, 2020)	Automatic Test Equipment	1 Donated surgical masks and personal protective equipment 2 Distributed free lunch and dinner for employees	1 Frontliners 2 employees
5	Kuala Lumpur Kepong *Berhad* (Kuala Lumpur Kepong *Berhad*, 2020)	i Plantation ii Oleochemical iii Property	1 Purchased of foods, personal protective equipment and medical supplies (RM6.6 million)	1 Employees, 2 Students, 3 B40 community, 4 Needy communities 5 Medical workers, police (Malaysia and Indonesia)
6	Fraser & Neave Holdings *Berhad* (Fraser & Neave Holdings *Berhad*, 2020)	Food and Beverages	1 Partnered with local councils to develop collaterals to increase awareness on COVID-19 prevention for 430 School across Malaysia (RM 400,000.00)	1 200 beneficiaries from vulnerable communities
7	UWC *Berhad* (UWC *Berhad*, 2020)	Fabrication Service	1 Contributed to Penang States Government and schools by donating hand sanitiser, and COVID-19 Screening Booth to Penang General Hospital	1 Penang States Government Schools 2 Penang General Hospital

8	VS Industry *Berhad* (VS Industry *Berhad*, 2020)	Manufacturing	1 Face mask (RM 53,000.00) 2 Foodbanks (RM 23,000.00)	1 3 Hospitals in JB 2 Kulai District Police 3 Headquarter, Senai Police Station 4 Kulai Municipal Council 5 B40 families
9	Nexgram Holdings *Berhad* (Nexgram Holdings *Berhad*, 2020)	i Information, Communication and Technology ii Property Based Business	Medical Surgical Mask	1 Frontliners for Negeri Melaka
10	Subur Tiasa Holdings *Berhad* (Subur Tiasa Holdings *Berhad*, 2020)	Wood-Based Manufacturing	Sponsorship for medical supplies	1 Frontliners-Kota Kinabalu, Kelantan, Sungai Buluh, Melaka
11	Scientex *Berhad* (Scientex *Berhad*, 2020)	i Producers of stretch film and a leading player in the flexible plastic packaging industry ii Home developer	1 Contributed for Clinical Trials (Partnership with UM Medical Center, Sungai Buluh Hospital, Kuala Lumpur Hospital and Tuanku Jaafar Hospital. (RM 300,000) 2 Donated customised plastic films use of wards partitions (RM 100,000) 3 Donated Medical 3-ply face masks to Ministry of Health (RM70,000)	1 Relief Funds-Kerajaan Negeri Melaka 2 Tabung Bencana Negeri Johor

(*Continued*)

Table 4.1 (Continued)

No.	*Company*	*Core business*	*Supports*	*Target respondents*
12	ProLexus *Berhad* (ProLexus *Berhad*, 2020)	Apparel manufacturing	1 Collaborated with DHL for distribution of reusable fabric face mask ProXMask to improve environmental awareness	1 School in Northern, Southern and Central region
13	JayCorp *Berhad* (JayCorp *Berhad*, 2020)	i Rubberwood manufacturing ii Packaging iii General trading iv Others	1 2500 Medical Protective Suits	1 Sabah State Government frontliners
14	Hiap Teck Venture *Berhad* (Hiap Teck Venture *Berhad*, 2020)	i Major Importer ii Steel Stockholder iii Distributor of structural steel products	1 Financial support to charitable organisations through donation and sponsorship 2 Contributed a total of RM500,000.00 to "The Edge COVID-19 Pandemic Funds" to help Malaysian healthcare system fight the COVID-19 crisis	1 Healthcare System

15	Top Glove Corporation *Berhad* (Top Glove Corporation *Berhad*, 2020)	Glove makers	1 A total of 3 million pieces of Glove Donation to China as a part of joint initiative between the Malaysian government and Malaysian glove makers 2 More than 4 million gloves were donated to various government Ministries, Royal Malaysian Police and Malaysian charity organisations 3 Medical Equipment Contribution: More than RM300,000 worth of ventilators and medical suits to the Ministry of Health Malaysia for frontliners and medical professionals 4 A total of 10,516 volunteer hours were contributed by staff for glove packing 5 A total of RM 5,000,000.00 spent	1 International (China) 2 Healthcare and Frontline 3 To those impacted by the pandemic
16	Gamuda *Berhad* (Gamuda *Berhad*, 2020)	Engineering and Construction	1 Upskilled and trained the women from Temuan Orang Asli to sew and sell reusable face mask	1 Community

(*Continued*)

Table 4.1 (*Continued*)

No.	*Company*	*Core business*	*Supports*	*Target respondents*
17	Seacera Group *Berhad* (Seacera Group *Berhad*, 2020)	Ceramic Industry	1 PPE products included the facemask, thermometer, and hand sanitiser for schools and mosque	1 Community
18	EG Industries *Berhad* (EG Industries *Berhad*, 2020)	Electronic Manufacturing Service	1 Donatied of necessities kit to frontliners	1 Police 2 Customs
19	Eden Inc. *Berhad* (Eden Inc. *Berhad*, 2020)	Management Service Company	1 The Food and Beverages department supported food supplies to the frontliners	1 Frontliners
20	Revenue Group *Berhad* (Revenue Group *Berhad*, 2020)	Payment Service	1 Organised a "revPAY Donation Drive" internally between 22 June 2020 to 24 June 2020 to raise fund for Thangam Illam Welfare Society (orphanage home) and Persatuan Kebajikan Dan Social Kim Loo Ting Kuala Lumpur (orphanage and old folks home) 2 A total of RM14,480 has been raised by kind-hearted employees including cash and essential goods presented and delivered to the two charitable organisations on 29 June 2020	1 Needy

21	Supermax Corporation *Berhad* (Supermax Corporation *Berhad*, 2020)	Latex glove conglomerate	1 Donated a total of 3 million gloves and co-sponsored a further 8.9 million gloves to China to aid them in their fight against the deadly virus 2 Donated and co-sponsored a total of 6 million gloves to the frontliners such as the doctors and nurses as well as the police and army personnel	1 Chinese people in China 2 Frontliners
22	Uzma *Berhad* (Uzma *Berhad*, 2020)	Oil and Gas Service and Equipment company	1 Food sponsorship to the community during the MCO via the Pertubuhan Sahabat Jariah 2 Contributed to the daily sustenance of communities that had been severely impacted by the COVID-19 pandemic, as a result of job losses or reductions in income 3 Collaborated with ANSARA Malaysia to provide medical equipment and supplies to Malaysian Relief Agency, hospitals, healthcare front liners and the needy	1 Community 2 Frontliners

(*Continued*)

Table 4.1 (*Continued*)

No.	*Company*	*Core business*	*Supports*	*Target respondents*
			4 Provided meals for frontliners at Hospital Serdang and Hospital Sungai Buloh 5 Provided meals for the homeless in collaboration with the NGO Need to Feed the Need at Dewan 6 Assisted the homeless communities, who had been further displaced during the MCO 7 Provided breaking fast meals for the homeless in collaboration with the NGO Need to Feed the Need at Dewan Serbaguna Ampang Hilir	
23	Kim Teck Cheong Consolidated *Berhad* (Kim Teck Cheong Consolidated *Berhad*, 2020)	First tier provider of market access and coverage in the distribution of Consumer Package Goods ("CPG") in East Malaysia	1 Donated a total of 10,000 loaves of bread to the nation's frontlines in support of the roadblock operations throughout the country 2 Donated a total of 5,000 loaves of bread during the MCO period to the Malaysian Volunteer Corps Department ("RELA")	1 Frontliners

24	Seremban Engineering *Berhad* (Seremban Engineering *Berhad*, 2020)	Engineering	1 Donated a total of six units of refurbished desktops to SJKC Chung Hua Seremban	1 SJKC Hua Seremban
25	Malton *Berhad* (Malton *Berhad*, 2020)	Property Developer	1 Donated personal protective equipment (PPE): included 500,000 pieces of surgical masks, safety glasses and full-body protective suits to our national heroes through the National Disaster Management Agency (NADMA) and Ministry of Health (MOH)	1 Frontliners
26	Borneo Oil *Berhad* (Borneo Oil *Berhad*, 2020)	i Food and Franchise Operations ii Property Investment and Management iii Resources and Sustainable Energy	1 Provided meal sponsorship for Miri General Hospital for Medical Front liners at with Collaboration SB Piasau 2 Provided meal sponsorship for Kota Kinabalu Army/Police front liners during MCO	1 Frontliners
27	Kwantas Corporation *Berhad* (Kwantas Corporation *Berhad*, 2020)	i Palm oil ii Plantations iii Manufacturing and Processing iv Biomass Power Plant	1 Sabah State Government Organised "We Care, We Love" Charity Dinner (Proceeds in aid of the Wuhan Crisis) within collaboration with several non-governmental organisations initiated a fund-raising campaign. A total of RM2 million were successfully raised	1 Affected Community

Table 4.2 The CSR contributions from companies in Malaysia

No.	*Company*	*Core business*	*Supports*	*Target respondents*
1	Tuck Sun Sdn Bhd (Tucksun.com, 2020)	Logistic Company	1 Donated of face shields to autistic children from NASOM (National Autistic Society of Malaysia) Klang 2 Donated of PPE to fellow households, schools and local businesses in our vicinity	1 Community/needy
2	Celcom Axiata *Berhad* (Bernama, 2020)	Telecommunication	1 Collaborated with Malaysian Relief Agency (MRA) since April to channel aid such as food supplies to the B40 group living in areas severely affected by COVID-19 in Sabah 2 Provided Internet plans for the use of the Ministry of Health (MOH) as well as XPAX prepaid SIM packs at quarantine centres nationwide	1 Community/needy
3	Digi.Com *Berhad* (Bernama, 2020)	Telecommunication	1 Introduced the Sabah Youth JENDELA package which includes NEXT Digital Prepaid products that offer unlimited Internet access and calls to all networks	1 Community/needy
4	Maxis *Berhad* (Bernama, 2020)	Telecommunication	1 Collaborated with MOH to provide connectivity services for hospitals and authorities; and the state governments to provide communication support particularly to the small and medium enterprises (SMEs) during the Conditional Movement Control Order (CMCO)	1 Community/needy 2 Frontliners
5	U Mobile Sdn Bhd (Bernama, 2020)	Telecommunication	1 Partnered with a public funding platform Hanafundme and collaborated with Huawei to sponsor 60 mobile devices complete with a GX68 postpaid plan for a period of one year to help Sabah school students	1 Students

6	Telecom Malaysia *Berhad* (Bernama, 2020)	Telecommunication	1 TM has provided 100 Mbps broadband service connection at Medan ATM Hospital in Tawau and 800 Mbps at PPR Bubul Ria quarantine centre in Semporna	1 Health Centre in Tawau and Semporna
7	TIME dotCom *Berhad* (Bernama, 2020)	Telecommunication	1 TIME dotcom has supported the purchase medical supplies, personal protective equipment (PPE) and ventilators	1 Health Centre
8	Siemens Malaysia Sdn. Bhd (Siemens Healthineers and Siemens Mobility) (Siemens Malaysia, 2020)	i Healthcare ii Transportation system	1 Distributed of the 2000 care packs comprised of beverages, biscuits, oatmeal and vitamin C to hospitals and police stations near their headquarters	1 University Malaya Medical Center 2 Kuala Lumpur General Hospital 3 Police Station Damansara and Tun Dr. Ismail
9	Plus Malaysia *Berhad* (Plus.com.my, 2020)	Expressway assets and liability	1 Contributed of RM1.2 million worth of medical supplies and personal protective equipment (PPE) to the Kuala Lumpur (HKL) and Sungai Buloh (HSB) hospitals to help combat the COVID-19 pandemic	1 Frontliners 2 COVID patients
10	KYY Home Sdn Bhd (The Star Online, 2020)	Property and management	1 A total CSR efforts are valued at RM2 million 2 Secured and distributed 50,000 face masks and hand sanitisers to its employees, tenants and business partners, giving them additional protection against the health threat 3 Introduced a special allowance of 15% to 20% on top of salaries to offer some temporary relief from financial strain for employees 4 Two months of rental subsidies to its tenants 5 Offered free accommodation to medical officers who have been transferred from other states to the Klang Valley	1 Customers/Tenant 2 Employees 3 Frontliners

(*Continued*)

Table 4.2 (Continued)

No.	*Company*	*Core business*	*Supports*	*Target respondents*
			6 Offered a Corporate Employee Housing Welfare Programme to help young employees secure a cost-effective housing loan from financial institutions to buy their property. Including, waive of the down payment, legal and documentation fees	
11	Pengurusan Air Selangor Sdn Bhd (British Malaysia Chamber of Commerce, 2020)	Water Distribution	1 Partneed with Village Grocer and Yayasan Food Bank Malaysia to encourage customers to donate essential food items to the special Air Selangor x Village Grocer's Box of Hope, those items will be distributed to various charities associated with Yayasan Food Bank 2 Introduced Plumbing Apprenticeship Programme for individual who are looking to reskill their current career 3 Introduced Air Selangor Plumbing Assistance Service for recipients with financial constraints and those in need for immediate plumbing repair 4 Introduced Animal adoption initiative with Zoo Negara 5 Introduced Special educational programme for employee's children	1 The needy/ community 2 Individual 3 Environment/ animals 4 Employees' children
12	Petroliam Nasional *Berhad* (Petronas) (Battersby, 2020)	Oil and Gas	1 Contributed medical equipment and supplies worth 20 million ringgit ($4.51 million) to help hospitals and frontline healthcare workers.	1 Hospital 2 Frontliners

13	Nestle (Malaysia) *Berhad* (Nestlé Malaysia, 2020)	Food and Beverages	1 Spent a total of RM15 million to support Malaysians during COVID-19 in the year of 2020 2 Collaborated with Empire Project NGO, Nestlé Cares Back-To-School Programme has donated school uniforms and supplies, as well as Nestlé products to over 1,100 low-income families 3 Partnered with the Malaysian Red Crescent Society (MRCS) to distribute food and beverage (F&B) products to help nourish frontliners and communities in need, along with a cash contribution of RM1 million to upgrade emergency medical equipment in MRCS ambulances 4 Sponsored over RM4.5 million worth of nutritious EVERYDAY products to over 85,000 Malaysians from vulnerable communities impacted by COVID-19, included PPR communities, charity homes, as well as to frontliners based in hospitals across Malaysia 5 Nestlé Malaysia has contributed more than RM541,000 in products and cash donations to more than 30,000 Sabahans, including frontliners as well as families and communities in need	1 Community/needy 2 Frontliners

(*Continued*)

Table 4.2 (Continued)

No.	*Company*	*Core business*	*Supports*	*Target respondents*
14.	Sime Darby Property (Simedarbyproperty.com, 2020)	Property	1 Donation on "COVID-19 Relief Aid for Schools in Need" included hygiene items such as hand sanitisers, face masks, infrared thermometers and disinfectant liquids were distributed to nine schools across the Klang Valley, Negeri Sembilan and Johor 2 As part of the internal Sime Darby Property Volunteers Programme (SDPVP), the Group also organised the "Be a Face Mask Maker with SURI Inspirasi" campaign where 30 of its employees lent their hands to make 5,000 reusable cloth face masks for underprivileged communities	1 Student 2 Teachers 3 The needy/ community
15.	Coway Malaysia (Business Today, 2020)	Water Treatment	1 Distributed of 10,000 sets of hand sanitisers and masks to GrabFood delivery customers of selected eatery outlets within greater Kuala Lumpur	1 Community
16.	7-Eleven Malaysia Holdings *Berhad* (Raj, 2020)	Retails Industry	1 Contributed more than RM1 million in essential items, such as test kits and PPEs, to various government bodies and NGOs nationwide	1 Community 2 Frontliners

and clinical trials. This shows how CSR has created a good support system for the Ministry of Health in combating the COVID-19.

Considering the employees as an important asset, the companies also offer CSR in terms of safety, medical, and financial support to tackle the welfare of the employees. MKH *Berhad*, for example, has invited doctors to conduct swab tests for all employees at the headquarters as a precautionary measure against COVID-19. This shows how employers appreciate their employees and concern for their safety. KYY Home Sdn Bhd sets another example of how the CSR activities by the company are beneficial to the employees. Through the Corporate Employee Housing Welfare Programme, the company helps young employees secure a cost-effective housing loan from financial institutions to buy their property. Including the waiver of the down payment, legal and documentation fees. This is another way to help the survival of the employees, especially during the economic recession due to COVID-19.

4.3.2 Customer relationships

As for the customer dimensions, it can be seen that most of the telecommunications companies such as XOX, Maxis, Celcom, Digi, UMobile, Telekom Malaysia offer their internet package to the customers and get benefits from free internet access. A total of RM6 million has been contributed by the telecommunications companies to the frontliners and public (locals) who have been unfavourably affected by the COVID-19 pandemic (Bernama, 2020). The internet has become intensely important after the new normal of working and studying from home. The CSR made by these telecommunication companies has been greatly appreciated and utilised by all Malaysians. This finding is in line with a study conducted by Servera-Francés and Piqueras-Tomás (2019) in which CSR policies increase trust, commitment, satisfaction, loyalty, and consumers' perceived value towards service providers.

4.3.3 Community and social engagement

The community and social dimensions show that the companies are highly concerned for their survival. They were supported with varieties of basic necessities, including foods, safety essentials (mask and sanitiser), personal development, and education. The companies have their own different target respondents to provide the support. There are companies that collaborate with the local agency, such as AHB *Berhad*, to deliver support/relief to the targeted respondents. The essential support is continuously happening during this critical time. Some companies open for collaboration with other parties to collect more funds for CSR, such as Revenue Group *Berhad*, Pengurusan Air Selangor Sdn. Bhd. and Kwantas Corporation *Berhad*.

Instead of just providing the financial support and basic necessities, there are companies that choose to offer personal development support through CSR programmes. The efforts from companies such as Gamuda *Berhad* to upskill and train the women from Temuan Orang Asli to sew and sell reusable face masks; *Pengurusan Air Selangor Sdn. Bhd* to introduce the Plumbing Apprenticeship Programme for individuals who are looking to reskill their current career and Special Educational Programme for employee's children to catch up the syllabus of their schools. This shows that CSR is not just supporting the basic necessities but upgrading the life of the needy. Along with the various support through donations and reliefs, some companies were concerned about the environment, especially the donation of reusable face masks. The use of reusable face masks is better for the environment as well as helping underprivileged communities.

4.3.4 Employees' volunteerism

Other than these dimensions, the CSR also can be successfully made from the volunteerism of the employees, such as the Sime Darby Property Volunteers Programme (SDPVP). The group of employees has also organised the "Be a Face Mask Maker with SURI Inspirasi" campaign, in which 30 of its employees lent their hands to make 5,000 reusable cloth face masks for underprivileged communities. In Top Glove, 10,516 volunteer hours were contributed by staff for glove packing. Hence, it is not a surprise when it can be seen that the CSR was also raised to the international level by Top Glove Corporation *Berhad* when it sent 3 million pieces of gloves to China as a part of joint initiative between the Malaysian government and Malaysian glove makers. This indicates that the employees are the important support system to the company for the success of CSR.

Overall, the findings reveal that the contributions of CSR from these companies are important to their stakeholders, including the frontliners, public health, employees, customers, and community. Although these companies have different target groups in delivering CSR facilities, it does address the dilemma of the needy. The needy are not just being supported through basic necessities but also for their personal development to survive. This supported the theoretical point of view by García-Sánchez and García-Sánchez (2020), in which most of the firms around the world focus only on specific interest groups within a short time and developed practices that pursue good common goals.

4.4 Conclusion

The emergence of COVID-19 has dramatically changed the world, whereby it swiftly and harshly interrupted life and economies, forcing businesses and governments to quickly make difficult choices to balance risks between individual health and economic health (Manuel and Herron, 2020). In view of the stakeholder theory, the companies have put their obligation in addressing the needs of the society by focusing on public health, survival of the society, education and many more. Although most of the CSR activities are peripheral, which is not related to their core business, the efforts have built a strong support system in combating the COVID-19 along with the government efforts. It can be seen that many organisations are making efforts to contribute to the societies' well-being, and every party has played their part very well. The employees in those organisations played a prominent role in the success of CSR. Future research should focus on how well the CSR activities are able to promote the financial stability and corporate image of the organisations as well as social well-being for the post-COVID-19.

Summary

- Many profit-oriented organisations in Malaysia have taken part in CSR during COVID-19 pandemic.
- The main group of target respondents for CSR is frontliners, employees, committee/local/underprivileged, and customers.
- Most of the CSR activities are peripheral which do not directly relate to the main core of the business.
- The focuses of CSR activities during COVID are public health, survival of the society, education, and others.
- The CSR activities include distribution of basic necessities, personal development of the communities and customer well-being.

References

AEMULUS Holdings *Berhad*. (2020). Annual Report. Available at https://www.malaysiastock.biz/Annual-Report.aspx [Accessed 29 January 2021].

AHB Group. (2020). Annual Report. Available at https://www.malaysiastock.biz/Annual-Report.aspx [Accessed 29 January 2021].

Bae, K. H., El Ghoul, S., Gong, Z. J., & Guedhami, O. (2021). Does CSR matter in times of crisis? Evidence from the COVID-19 pandemic. *Journal of Corporate Finance*, *67*, 101876.

Battersby, A. (2020). *Petronas Stumps up Millions for COVID-19 Help | Upstream Online*. [online] Upstream Online | Latest oil and gas news. Available at: https://

www.upstreamonline.com/coronavirus/petronas-stumps-up-millions-for-COVID-19-help/2-1-780502 [Accessed 14 February 2021].

Bernama (2020). *Telcos Contribute RM6m to Frontliners, Locals Affected by COVID-19*. [online] The Malaysian Reserve. Available at: https://themalaysianreserve.com/2020/11/05/telcos-contribute-rm6m-to-frontliners-locals-affected-by-COVID-19/ [Accessed 13 February 2021].

Borneo Oil *Berhad*. (2020). Annual Report. Available at https://www.malaysiastock.biz/Annual-Report.aspx [Accessed 29 January 2021].

British Malaysia Chamber of Commerce. (2020). *Village Grocer joins Air Selangor #Sesamamara CSR Programme | British Malaysian Chamber of Commerce (BMCC)*. [online] Available at: https://www.bmcc.org.my/vault/news/village-grocer-joins-air-selangor-sesamamara-csr-programme [Accessed 9 February 2021].

Brin, P. V., & Nehme, M.N. (2019). Corporate social responsibility: analysis of theories and models. *EUREKA: Social and Humanities*, *5*, 22–30.

Bursa Malaysia. (2021). *Listing on Bursa Saham*. [online] Available at: https://www.bursamalaysia.com/listing/get_listed/listing_criteria [Accessed 13 February 2021].

Business Today. (2020). *Coway Gives Away 10,000 Masks and Sanitisers to Grabfood Customers - Business Today*. [online] Available at: https://www.businesstoday.com.my/2020/03/26/coway-gives-away-10000-masks-and-sanitisers-for-grabfood-customers/ [Accessed 14 February 2021].

Ducharme, J. (2020). *The WHO Just Declared Coronavirus COVID-19 a Pandemic*. [online] Time. Available at: https://time.com/5791661/who-coronavirus-pandemic-declaration/ [Accessed 12 February 2021].

Ding, W., Levine, R., Lin, C., & Xie, W. (2020). *Corporate Immunity to the COVID-19 Pandemic* (No. w27055). National Bureau of Economic Research.

Eden Inc. *Berhad*. (2020). Annual Report. Available at https://www.malaysiastock.biz/Annual-Report.aspx [Accessed 29 January 2021].

EG Industries *Berhad*. (2020). Annual Report. Available at https://www.malaysiastock.biz/Annual-Report.aspx [Accessed 29 January 2021].

Elo, S., Kääriäinen, M., Kanste, O., Pölkki, T., Utriainen, K., & Kyngäs, H. (2014). Qualitative content analysis: A focus on trustworthiness. *SAGE Open*, *4*(1), 1–10.

Filimonau, V., Derqui, B., & Matute, J. (2020). The COVID-19 pandemic and organisational commitment of senior hotel managers. *International Journal of Hospitality Management*, *91*, 102659.

Fraser & Neave Holdings *Berhad*. (2020). Annual Report. Available at https://www.malaysiastock.biz/Annual-Report.aspx [Accessed 29 January 2021].

Freeman, R. E. (2015). Stakeholder theory. *Wiley Encyclopedia of Management*, 1–6. DOI:10.1002/9781118785317.weom020179

Gamuda *Berhad*. (2020). Annual Report. Available at https://www.malaysiastock.biz/Annual-Report.aspx [Accessed 29 January 2021].

García-Sánchez, I. M., & García-Sánchez, A. (2020). Corporate social responsibility during COVID-19 pandemic. *Journal of Open Innovation: Technology, Market, and Complexity*, *6*(4), 126.

Gatti, L., Vishwanath, B., Seele, P., & Cottier, B. (2019). Are we moving beyond voluntary CSR? Exploring theoretical and managerial implications of mandatory

CSR resulting from the new Indian companies act. *Journal of Business Ethics*, *160*(4), 961–972.

Graneheim, U. H., Lindgren, B. M., & Lundman, B. (2017). Methodological challenges in qualitative content analysis: A discussion paper. *Nurse Education Today*, *56*, 29–34.

He, H., & Harris, L. (2020). The impact of COVID-19 pandemic on corporate social responsibility and marketing philosophy. *Journal of Business Research*, *116*, 176–182.

Johns Hopkins Coronavirus Resource Center. (2021). *Home - Johns Hopkins Coronavirus Resource Center*. [online] Available at: https://coronavirus.jhu.edu [Accessed 12 February 2021].

Hiap Teck Venture *Berhad*. (2020). Annual Report. Available at https://www.malaysiastock.biz/Annual-Report.aspx [Accessed 29 January 2021].

JayCorp *Berhad*. (2020). Annual Report. Available at https://www.malaysiastock.biz/Annual-Report.aspx [Accessed 29 January 2021].

Kim, M., Yin, X., & Lee, G. (2020). The effect of CSR on corporate image, customer citizenship behaviors, and customers' long-term relationship orientation. *International Journal of Hospitality Management*, *88*, 102520.

Kim Teck Cheong Consolidated *Berhad*. (2020). Annual Report. Available at https://www.malaysiastock.biz/Annual-Report.aspx [Accessed 29 January 2021].

Kuala Lumpur Kepong *Berhad*. (2020). Annual Report. Available at https://www.malaysiastock.biz/Annual-Report.aspx [Accessed 29 January 2021].

Kwantas Corporation *Berhad*. (2020). Annual Report. Available at https://www.malaysiastock.biz/Annual-Report.aspx [Accessed 29 January 2021].

Malaysiastock.biz. (2021). *Latest Annual Reports | MalaysiaStock.Biz*. [online] Available at: https://www.malaysiastock.biz/Annual-Report.aspx [Accessed 1 February 2021].

Malton *Berhad*. (2020). Annual Report. Available at https://www.malaysiastock.biz/Annual-Report.aspx [Accessed 29 January 2021].

Manuel, T., & Herron, T. L. (2020). An ethical perspective of business CSR and the COVID-19 pandemic. *Society and Business Review*. DOI: 10.1108/SBR-06-2020-0086

Mao, Y., He, J., Morrison, A. M., & Andres Coca-Stefaniak, J. (2020). Effects of tourism CSR on employee psychological capital in the COVID-19 crisis: From the perspective of conservation of resources theory. *Current Issues in Tourism*, 1–19. https://doi.org/10.1080/13683500.2020.1770706

Marom, S., & Lussier, R. N. (2020). Corporate social responsibility during the coronavirus pandemic: An interim overview. *Business and Economic Research*, *10*(2), 250–269.

MKH *Berhad*. (2020). Annual Report. Available at https://www.malaysiastock.biz/Annual-Report.aspx [Accessed 29 January 2021].

Nestlé Malaysia. (2020). *Our Response to COVID-19*. [online] Available at: https://www.nestle.com.my/impact-areas/our-response-COVID-19 [Accessed 12 February 2021].

Nexgram Holdings *Berhad*. (2020). Annual Report. Available at https://www.malaysiastock.biz/Annual-Report.aspx [Accessed 29 January 2021].

Plus.com.my. (2020). *Corporate Social Responsibility.* [online] Available at: https://www.plus.com.my/index.php?option=com_content&view=article&id=767&Itemid=378&lang=en [Accessed 11 February 2021].

ProLexus *Berhad.* (2020). Annual Report. Available at https://www.malaysiastock.biz/Annual-Report.aspx [Accessed 29 January 2021].

Qiu, S. C., Jiang, J., Liu, X., Chen, M. H., & Yuan, X. (2021). Can corporate social responsibility protect firm value during the COVID-19 pandemic?. *International Journal of Hospitality Management, 93*, 1027.

Radzi, N. A. M., Lee, K. E., Hashim, H., Ali, A. F. M., Saidi, N. A., & Hasbollah, H. R. (2020). Charity sees the need, not the cause: The strategic CSR during the pandemic outbreak. *PalArch's Journal of Archaeology of Egypt/Egyptology, 17*(4), 485–498.

Raj, M. (2020). *7-Eleven Malaysia Takes Home CSR Malaysia Award for Fourth Consecutive Year | Malay Mail.* [online] Malaymail.com. Available at: https://www.malaymail.com/news/life/2020/12/18/7-eleven-malaysia-takes-home-csr-malaysia-award-for-fourth-consecutive-year/1933178 [Accessed 14 February 2021].

Revenue Group *Berhad.* (2020). Annual Report. Available at https://www.malaysiastock.biz/Annual-Report.aspx [Accessed 29 January 2021].

Scientex *Berhad.* (2020). Annual Report. Available at https://www.malaysiastock.biz/Annual-Report.aspx [Accessed 29 January 2021].

Seacera Group *Berhad.* (2020). Annual Report. Available at https://www.malaysiastock.biz/Annual-Report.aspx [Accessed 29 January 2021].

Seremban Engineering *Berhad.* (2020). Annual Report. Available at https://www.malaysiastock.biz/Annual-Report.aspx [Accessed 29 January 2021].

Servera-Francés, D., & Piqueras-Tomás, L. (2019). The effects of corporate social responsibility on consumer loyalty through consumer perceived value. *Economic Research-Ekonomska istraživanja, 32*(1), 66–84.

Siemens Malaysia. (2020). *COVID-19 CSR | Features and stories | Malaysia.* [online] Available at: https://new.siemens.com/my/en/company/articles/features-and-stories/COVID-19-csr.html [Accessed 12 February 2021].

Simedarbyproperty.com. (2020). *Sime Darby Property.* [online] Available at: https://www.simedarbyproperty.com/press-releases/sime-darby-property-remains-committed-fighting-COVID-19-pandemic-safeguarding [Accessed 14 February 2021].

Subur Tiasa Holdings *Berhad.* (2020). Annual Report. Available at https://www.malaysiastock.biz/Annual-Report.aspx [Accessed 29 January 2021].

Supermax Corporation *Berhad.* (2020). Annual Report. Available at https://www.malaysiastock.biz/Annual-Report.aspx [Accessed 29 January 2021].

Tang, A. (2020). *Malaysia Announces Movement Control Order after Spike in COVID-19 cases (updated).* [online] The Star Online. Available at: https://www.thestar.com.my/news/nation/2020/03/16/malaysia-announces-restricted-movement-measure-after-spike-in-COVID-19-cases [Accessed 13 February 2021].

Tee, K. (2020). *Dr Noor Hisham: Malaysia Records Zero Local COVID-19 Transmissions for the Second Time, Three Imported Cases | Malay Mail.* [online] Malaymail.com. Available at: https://www.malaymail.com/news/malaysia/2020/07/08/dr-noor-hisham-malaysia-records-zero-local-COVID-19-transmissions-for-the-s/1882682 [Accessed 13 February 2021].

The Star Online. (2020). *CSR on Hyperdrive during Pandemic.* [online] Available at: https://www.thestar.com.my/news/nation/2020/05/15/csr-on-hyperdrive-during-pandemic [Accessed 12 February 2021].

Top Glove Corporation *Berhad.* (2020). Annual Report. Available at https://www.malaysiastock.biz/Annual-Report.aspx [Accessed 29 January 2021].

Tucksun.com. (2020). *COVID-19 Pandemic Relief – Tuck Sun Logistics.* [online] Available at: http://www.tucksun.com/COVID-19-pandemic-relief/ [Accessed 12 February 2021].UWC *Berhad.* (2020). Annual Report. Available at https://www.malaysiastock.biz/Annual-Report.aspx [Accessed 29 January 2021].

Uzma *Berhad.* (2020). Annual Report. Available at https://www.malaysiastock.biz/Annual-Report.aspx [Accessed 29 January 2021].

VS Industry *Berhad.* (2020). Annual Report. Available at https://www.malaysiastock.biz/Annual-Report.aspx [Accessed 29 January 2021].

XOX *Berhad.* (2020). Annual Report. Available at https://www.malaysiastock.biz/Annual-Report.aspx [Accessed 29 January 2021].

Zhang, Y., Diao, X., Chen, K. Z., Robinson, S., & Fan, S. (2020). Impact of COVID-19 on China's macroeconomy and agri-food system – an economy-wide multiplier model analysis. *China Agricultural Economic Review*, *12*(3), pp. 387–407.

5 The impact of COVID-19 on human capital in Malaysia

Insight from employers and employees

Lin Dar Ong and Su Teng Lee

5.1 Introduction

The Coronavirus disease (COVID-19) pandemic has posed unprecedented challenges to employees worldwide, leading to changes in their work behaviours, family experiences, and personal well-being (e.g., Kramer & Kramer, 2020; Trougakos et al., 2020; Vaziri et al., 2020). The crisis has revealed a gap in existing applied psychology research on large-scale and prolonged disruptive events (Yuan et al., 2020). Most press and research focused on the effects of the COVID-19 pandemic on workers' lives in developed nations (Fouad, 2020).

However, there has been less discussion about what happens to the jobs and experience of workers in developing countries, such as Malaysia. Furthermore, there is a lack of literature that focuses on practice-focused insights and recommendations for employers in Malaysia. This chapter discusses the past and current situation of the COVID-19 pandemic in Malaysia, as well as how the crisis affected both employers and employees in Malaysia. We also outline the ways in which employers and employees in Malaysia may adapt to "the new normal".

5.2 Literature review

The first case of highly contagious COVID-19 was reported in the People's Republic of China in December 2019. As the outbreak posed a major international threat, the World Health Organization (WHO) declared the COVID-19 outbreak a "Public Health Emergency of International Concern" (PHEIC) on 30 January 2020 (World Health Organization, 2020a).

According to BERNAMA.com (2020b), the first confirmed cases of COVID-19 in Malaysia involved three Chinese nationals from Wuhan who had entered Malaysia via Johor from Singapore on 23 January 2020. To stem the spread of the COVID-19 pandemic, Prime Minister Tan Sri Muhyiddin Yassin announced the implementation of the Movement Control Order

DOI: 10.4324/9781003182740-5

(MCO) starting from 18 March 2020. After several months, the government began to loosen the standard operating procedures (SOPs) with the introduction of the conditional MCO (CMCO) on 4 May 2020. As the cases went down, the government introduced more relaxation of restrictions through the Recovery MCO (RMCO) from 10 June 2020.

With the number of infections on the rise several months later, the government had to reimpose the CMCO in several states starting from 14 October 2020. As the pandemic swept rapidly across the country again at the beginning of 2021, the government had to implement MCO for the second time on 13 January 2021. On 30 January 2021, Malaysia reported a record high of 5728 new cases of COVID-19. As of 12 April 2021, 1333 people have died, and 362,173 confirmed COVID-19 cases have been in Malaysia since the start of the pandemic. As shown in Table 5.1, Malaysia now has the third-highest number of total COVID-19 cases in Southeast Asia, after Indonesia and the Philippines. The government has imposed travel and movement curbs to contain the spread of the virus.

Since the COVID-19 outbreak, working from home has become the new norm in Malaysia. According to a study on the COVID-19 pandemic's impact on the Malaysian workforce by a market research firm, Ipsos, 65% of Malaysians surveyed between 20 November and 4 December 2020 worked from home, compared to the 52% global average. The findings were released on 20 January 2021. In this study, Malaysians reported the highest level of anxiety among 28 countries surveyed for the study. More than half of Malaysian respondents (57%) said they felt lonely while

Table 5.1 Number of COVID-19 cases and deaths in the Southeast Asia region (as of April 9, 2021)

Countries	*Cases*	*Deaths*
Indonesia	1,558,145	42,348
Philippines	840,554	14,520
Malaysia	357,607	1,313
Myanmar	142,558	3,206
China	101,998	4,843
Singapore	60,601	30
Thailand	30,869	96
Cambodia	3,604	24
Vietnam	2,683	35
Timor Leste	877	1
Brunei	216	3
Laos	49	0

Source: The Center for Strategic and International Studies (CSIS). Available at: https://www.csis.org/programs/southeast-asia-program/southeast-asia-covid-19-tracker-0 (Accessed: 12 April 2021).

working from home. Sixty-three per cent of Malaysian workers find it difficult to achieve a work-life balance, while 62% have difficulty getting work done at home due to inadequate home office setup or equipment. In another survey by Randstad Malaysia, which was conducted in October 2020, revealed that 48% of 400 local respondents wanted a combination of working from home and the office after the COVID-19 pandemic. A further 14% of respondents want to work from home all the time (BERNAMA.com, 2021).

The COVID-19 crisis continued to hamper business, and many employees lost their jobs and incomes. According to the Malaysian Department of Statistics, the unemployment rate increased to 4.8% in November 2020 from 4.7% in October 2020, with 764,400 people unemployed as of November 2020. In December 2020, Emir Research conducted a state-wide survey with 1976 respondents nationwide. According to its survey, potential job loss remains Malaysians' top concern amid the ongoing COVID-19 pandemic, with nearly eight out of ten Malaysians expressing this fear. Furthermore, 81% of those polled expressed concern about losing their jobs as a result of the pandemic. In terms of household income, respondents earning between RM3001 and RM5000 appeared to be the most concerned, exhibiting significantly higher levels of concern about employment and living costs than those earning less than RM3000 overall (Tee, 2021).

According to BERNAMA.com (2020a), Tan Sri Lee said that 465 suicide attempts were reported by the Ministry of Health (MOH) between January and June 2020. He also stated that, despite the fact that the situation had improved with the implementation of RMCO, statistics from The Befrienders Kuala Lumpur suggested otherwise. This is because more calls from people in distress and contemplating suicide were received in July, August, and September than in April and May. Since the implementation of MCO in 2020, the Health Ministry has received over 43,000 calls to its psychosocial support hotline (BERNAMA.com, 2020c). The helpline is manned by the ministry's psychology officers and Mercy Malaysia volunteers. The government is also providing the Talian Kasih 15999 and Talian Khas Kaunseling COVID-19 hotlines via the Women, Family, and Community Development Ministry. The majority of the issues raised from the calls involve distress caused by job or income loss, lifestyle changes, family conflicts, and relationship issues.

Befrienders Kuala Lumpur, a non-profit organisation, also offers emotional support to anyone who is distressed and suicidal through their 24-hour helpline or email. Between 1 January and 21 January 2020, Befrienders received a total of 2240 calls. The majority of the concerns raised have to do with mental health, relationships, and employment. Health director-general Tan Sri Noor Hisham Abdullah stated that even with the vaccination plan in place, the number of calls is expected to remain high because many people are concerned about the vaccine's efficacy and safety (Yuen, 2021).

5.3 Methodology

The purpose of this chapter is to provide some useful insights and recommendations for employers and employees in Malaysia to cope with the novel COVID-19 pandemic. We reviewed various articles from academic literature and practice publications, such as newspaper articles, to provide a number of pragmatic recommendations that could be adopted by most organisations in Malaysia during the COVID-19 crisis.

5.3.1 Research design

The purpose of this chapter is to outline and explore the impact of COVID-19 on human capital in Malaysia. The chapter is based on practical rationality that is supported by informed findings from the existing literature and publicly available sources of information (e.g., daily news and governmental reports) to achieve the objective of this chapter. The main advantage of adopting secondary research is the ease of access to the latest information, as most of the information was available during the pandemic. Hence, secondary research offers the fastest access to the most up-to-date information with regards to the COVID-19 crisis in Malaysia.

5.3.2 Information collection method

Content analysis was used in this study. Current insights and ways forward for employers and employees were highlighted based on the inferences made from recent literature. During the COVID-19 pandemic, it was a widely used method for providing up-to-date insight into issues and best practices. We reviewed secondary content published in 2020 and 2021.

A number of relevant literature published were reviewed. The primary references used include local and international newspapers, government and WHO reports, and journal articles, which are related to the issues confronting employers and employees in the midst of the COVID-19 pandemic. Information gathering was carried out during the MCO 2.0 and MCO 3.0 periods in 2021. We also gathered and reviewed recent publications on good practices. Articles were examined, conceptualised and categorised into concepts as recommended by Hammersley and Atkinson (1983). It is a way to identify possible phenomena and divergence of views given by different parties.

5.3.3 *Lincoln and Guba's evaluative criteria*

According to Lincoln and Guba's (1985) evaluation criteria, trustworthiness is critical in evaluating research. It can be established through credibility, transferability, dependability, and confirmability. *Credibility* refers to the truthfulness of findings. *Transferability* refers to its application in other situations and contexts. *Dependability* means consistent findings and can be repeated. Lastly, *confirmability* refers to neutrality and is not based on researchers' biases and preferences. These were achieved through triangulation of sources where examination of the consistency of various data sources within the context was used. For instance, different references (newspapers, reports, and journal articles) were interpreted. Finally, various perspectives were used to examine and interpret the data to ensure dependability and confirmability. In this chapter, we ensure that most of the criteria for qualitative research outlined by Lincoln and Guba (1985) were met.

5.4 Findings

5.4.1 *The impact of the COVID-19 pandemic and recommendations for employers and employees in Malaysia*

Every employer and employee in Malaysia must understand the serious threats and dangers posed by the COVID-19 crisis and take precautions to ensure their safety and well-being at all times. The following subsections summarise the impact of the COVID-19 pandemic and the recommendations for employers and employees in Malaysia.

5.4.1.1 *Impact and recommendations for employers*

Companies have a moral and legal obligation to keep their employees and customers safe. To ensure COVID-safe workplaces, employers should take care of their employees and the workplaces. They must strictly enforce COVID-19 workplace regulations and abide by the nationwide general requirements for workplaces to mitigate the risk of widespread COVID-19 transmission. Table 5.2 lists some changes to expect in the post-COVID-19 workplace and several ways employers can take to create a COVID-19 free workplace.

5.4.1.2 *Impact and recommendations for employees*

As COVID-19 cases continue to rise, many people are stressed out and burned out. The COVID-19 pandemic can affect people physically, emotionally, spiritually, or psychologically. It has massively changed how

Table 5.2 Summary of the COVID-19 impacts and recommendations for employers

Impact	*Recommendations*
1 A large, permanent increase in remote work	• Implement policies and practices such as flexible work environments (e.g., telecommuting) and flexible work hours (e.g., work shifts) • Provide employees with some options: work remotely or face-to-face based on their nature of work and team' preferences • Encourage employees to leverage the use of technology to conduct virtual meetings internally and with external parties • Provide the specific tools, equipment, supplies, and technology needed for employees to perform the required tasks at home • Consider reimbursing employees for reasonable and necessary home office expenses, such as internet costs and laptops • Provide necessary training to employees to help them when working from home. For example, train them to use tools such as Google Meet, Microsoft Teams, Skype, Zoom, and WhatsApp
2 Continue operating safely during the COVID-19 pandemic	• Perform daily body temperature measurement and symptom screening on employees, visitors, and clients before allowing them to enter the workplace • Increase the physical distance between employees to six feet • Make sure that everyone is wearing masks and using hand sanitisers • Provide employees with appropriate PPE based on their needs. • Monitor control and prevention measures, including isolation of employees with COVID-19 symptoms • Maintain good housekeeping by cleaning and disinfecting surfaces, equipment, and other elements of the work environment on a regular and frequent basis • Provide targeted testing of new employees or those returning from a long absence, such as medical leave or furlough • Provide quarantine centres to isolate foreign workers who are confirmed COVID-19 positive • Provide COVID-19 screening tests for all foreign workers. • Ensures that COVID-19-related information, training, and supervision are provided and disseminated • Encourage staff to take the COVID-19 vaccine when it is offered • Have a dedicated COVID-19 Emergency Preparedness and Response Team that will plan, implement, and audit safe work procedures

(Continued)

Table 5.2 (Continued)

Impact	*Recommendations*
3 Maintain a high-performance work system	• Provide an Employee Assistance Program (EAP) or free counselling services to employees to assist them in resolving personal issues that may be interfering with their work performance • Set and communicate clear goals and reasonable deadlines to employees • Grant employees the right to disconnect during non-work hours. Do not abuse employees by making them work the entire day at home, as they are entitled to rest breaks under national legislation, collective agreements, or the company's terms and conditions of employment • Get feedback from employees and identify any areas for improvement • Manage work expectations, offer support, and take time to understand the unique needs of every employee
4 New guidelines set by the government	• Report to the Ministry of Health (MOH) immediately if any employees are found positive for COVID-19 • Fully comply with safety procedures introduced by the Occupational Safety and Health Department (DOSH) • Follow the most recent COVID-19 SOPs issued by the government • Check that the workplace is registered with the MySejahtera application • Provide a safe and comfortable workers' hostel in accordance with the Workers' Minimum Standards of Housing and Amenities Act of 1990

employees work, learn, communicate, and where they work. Table 5.3 lists the impact of the COVID-19 crisis on employees' lives, and some of the steps employees can take to stay well and recharge during the outbreak.

5.5 Conclusion

The COVID-19 pandemic created havoc on every level. In Malaysia alone, more than 1300 people have died, and around 100,000 people have lost their jobs due to the spread of COVID-19. The crisis forced companies to make numerous changes and called for an overhaul of HR and workplace safety practices. A combination of continued efforts to mitigate the spread of the virus and the rollout of vaccines under the National COVID-19 Immunisation Programme will eventually subdue the COVID-19 outbreak, but this will take some time. To weather the impact of COVID-19 in the months ahead, the government, businesses and individual workers

Table 5.3 Summary of the COVID-19 impacts and recommendations for employees

Impact	*Recommendations*
1 Adjust to work from home arrangement or the hybrid model	• Follow the company's information technology policy • Have a designated workspace at home and manage interruptions • Be available and accessible to their manager and coworkers during agreed-upon work hours • Maintain the same level of productivity and work quality when working from home • Notify immediate supervisor in the event of any emergency, including illness, injury, power outage, or loss of Internet connectivity. This is important as both employees and supervisors are physically apart, and they do not see each other face-to-face
2 The COVID-19-related rules and directives in the workplace	• Follow SOPs, which include making a self-declaration of health status and wearing required PPE while at work • Wear a face mask and a face shield when doing work that involves interaction with others in public and crowded places • Employees with COVID-19 symptoms must stay at home and promptly notify their supervisor • Follow any COVID-19-related rules and directives issued by your employer, as well as any government guidelines • Maintain a physical distance with others, stop shaking hands, and wash hands regularly • Attend safety briefing sessions related to control and preventive measures related to COVID-19 • Avoid unnecessary physical meetings and work activities that necessitate travel away from the office
3 Physical and mental well-being	• Limit multitasking during meetings • Disconnect or switch-off during non-work hours to avoid overwork • Block time on the calendar for exercise and fresh air—or just time to step away from the workspace • Check on others within your own community • Seek help and talk to others if you are stressed, depressed, or anxious. It is beneficial to discuss and share problems with a trusted coworker or supervisor • Keep up to date with the latest information from the Ministry of Health (MOH), the World Health Organization (WHO), or any other reliable source and act accordingly • Maintain a healthy lifestyle by doing things like meditation or prayer, exercising, eating a healthy diet and sticking to a sleep schedule

have a shared responsibility to work together and make sacrifices to minimise COVID-19 disruption and long-term unemployment.

Summary

- All employers and employees must follow the safety and health guidelines issued by the authorities with regard to COVID-19.
- Every employer should communicate clear goals to all employees who work from home and regulate the right for employees to disconnect during non-work hours.
- Employers must ensure employees and visitors are protected in the workplace.
- Every employee should maintain a healthy lifestyle and prevent remote-work flexibility from sliding into overwork.
- Everyone should do their part by observing safe distancing and practising good personal hygiene to reduce the risk of transmission.

References

BERNAMA.com (2021). Half of Malaysian workers want flexible work arrangements post-pandemic—survey. The Edge Markets. [Online]. Available at: https://www.theedgemarkets.com/article/half-malaysian-workers-want-flexible-work-arrangements-postpandemic-%E2%80%94-survey (Accessed: 30 April 2021).

BERNAMA.com (2020a). Survey finds almost half a million Malaysians experience symptoms of depression [Online]. Available at: https://www.bernama.com/en/general/news.php?id=1888427 (Accessed: 30 April 2021).

BERNAMA.com (2020b). COVID-19 chronology in Malaysia [Online]. Available at: https://www.bernama.com/en/general/news_covid-19.php?id=1821902 (Accessed: 30 April 2021).

BERNAMA.com (2020c). Health Ministry received over 43,000 calls for help since MCO started. [Online]. Available at: https://www.bernama.com/en/general/news_covid-19.php?id=1912851 (Accessed: 30 April 2021).

Fouad, N. A. (2020). Editor in chief's introduction to essays on the impact of COVID-19 on work and workers. *Journal of Vocational Behavior*, *119*, 103441.

Hammersley, M., & Atkinson, P. (1983). *Ethnography: Principles in Practice.* London: Tavistock.

Kramer, A., & Kramer, K. Z. 2020. The potential impact of the Covid-19 pandemic on occupational status, work from home, and occupational mobility. *Journal of Vocational Behavior*, *119*, 103442.

Lincoln, Y. S., & Guba, E. G. (1985). *Naturalistic Inquiry.* Newbury Park, CA: Sage.

Tee, K. (2021). Emir Research: Over eight in 10 Malaysians still fear losing jobs to Covid-19 pandemic. MalayMail, 8 February [online]. Available at: https://www.malaymail.com/news/malaysia/2021/02/08/survey-over-eight-in-10-malaysians-still-fear-losing-jobs-to-covid-19-pande/1947962 (Accessed: 30 April 2021).

The Center for Strategic and International Studies (CSIS). Southeast Asia Covid-19 tracker. Available at: https://www.csis.org/programs/southeast-asia-program/southeast-asia-covid-19-tracker-0 (Accessed: 12 April 2021).

Trougakos, J. P., Chawla, N., & McCarthy, J. M. (2020). Working in a pandemic: Exploring the impact of COVID-19 health anxiety on work, family, and health outcomes. *Journal of Applied Psychology*, *105*(11), 1234.

Vaziri, H., Casper, W. J., Wayne, J. H., & Matthews, R. A. (2020). Changes to the work–family interface during the COVID-19 pandemic: Examining predictors and implications using latent transition analysis. *Journal of Applied Psychology*, *105*(10), 1073.

World Health Organization (2020a). Statement on the second meeting of the International Health Regulations (2005) Emergency Committee regarding the outbreak of novel coronavirus (2019-nCoV) [Online]. Available at: https://www.who.int/news/item/30-01-2020-statement-on-the-second-meeting-of-the-international-health-regulations-(2005)-emergency-committee-regarding-the-outbreak-of-novel-coronavirus-(2019-ncov) (Accessed: 30 April 2021).

World Health Organization (2020). Mental health and COVID-19. https://www.euro.who.int/en/health-topics/health-emergencies/coronavirus-covid-19/publications-and-technical-guidance/noncommunicable-diseases/mental-health-and-covid-19 (Accessed: 30 April 2021).

Yuan, Z., Ye, Z., & Zhong, M. (2020). Plug back into work, safely: Job reattachment, leader safety commitment, and job engagement in the COVID-19 pandemic. *Journal of Applied Psychology*, *106*(1), 62–70.

Yuen, M. (2021). More calls for help in MCO 2.0. The Star, 7 February [online]. Available at: https://www.thestar.com.my/news/focus/2021/02/07/more-calls-for-help-in-mco-20 (Accessed: 30 April 2021).

6 The impact of COVID-19 on public policy in Malaysia

Insights from the loan moratorium and the hospitality industry

Siti Nurhayati Khairatun

6.1 Introduction

In March 2020, the Government of Malaysia announced the implementation of a Movement Control Order (MCO) as an effort to flatten the infection curve of COVID-19 due to escalating positive cases in the country. As of today, Malaysia has experienced two rounds of MCO with a series of orders that restrict people from travelling abroad, inter-state or inter-district movement. The first round of MCO started on March 18, 2020, until December 30, 2020, with several renewals and extensions of orders (see Figure 6.1). The second round of MCO was declared to begin on January 13, 2021, until March 18, 2021. In the first round of MCO, most public and private sectors were ordered to work from home except for those who were involved in essential services. After a couple of months under partial lockdown, Malaysia had lifted the MCO and replaced it with various orders in stages to relax the restrictions. Under the first phase of MCO, only certain sectors categorised as essential could continue operating with strict observation of specific standard operating procedures (SOP). Other than essential services, businesses, and manufacturing sectors, they should halt operation temporarily until the government issued them a special approval to resume their operation.

Food-related businesses, including food retail, food service business, and restaurants, are considered essential sectors because the public should be able to get access to sufficient, healthy, and affordable food supply during the lockdown. During the first phase of MCO, customers were not allowed to dine-in within the restaurant premises as all orders must be done by take-away, drive-through, or delivered by food riders only. Operating hours were limited to 8 am until 6 pm only. Later, when the MCO was relaxed, restaurants were allowed to operate longer hours, to have their customers dine-in with strict observation of SOP including the requirements for customers to wear the mask, to have temperature measured and

DOI: 10.4324/9781003182740-6

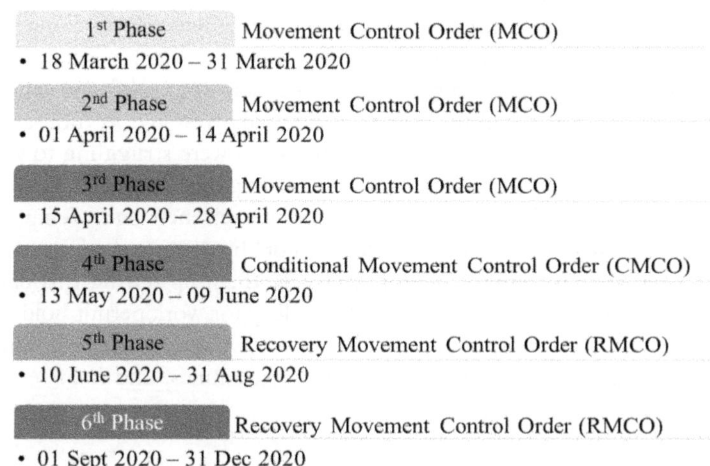

1st Phase
Movement Control Order (MCO)
• 18 March 2020 – 31 March 2020
2nd Phase
Movement Control Order (MCO)
• 01 April 2020 – 14 April 2020
3rd Phase
Movement Control Order (MCO)
• 15 April 2020 – 28 April 2020
4th Phase
Conditional Movement Control Order (CMCO)
• 13 May 2020 – 09 June 2020
5th Phase
Recovery Movement Control Order (RMCO)
• 10 June 2020 – 31 Aug 2020
6th Phase
Recovery Movement Control Order (RMCO)
• 01 Sept 2020 – 31 Dec 2020

Figure 6.1 The rounds of Movement Control Orders (MCOs) 2020 in Malaysia

personal details recorded using the MySejahtera app, to apply sanitiser and to observe one-meter distancing between diners. All these measures have discouraged customer turnover at restaurants. According to the Malaysian Muslim Restaurant Owners Association (Presma), the members' restaurant businesses have lost about 80% of revenues from the pandemic lockdown as most customers preferred to stay at home (Azman, 2020). Data from SYCARDA estimated restaurants had lost about 90% of their revenues during the lockdown between March and April 2020 compared to the same period the previous year (Malay Mail, 2020).

The implementation of economic closures in the first round and second round of MCO are distinguished as more economies were allowed to operate during the second round of MCO. During the first round of MCO, many restaurants have suffered financially and decided to close their businesses permanently. For some, they are still thriving in survival mode with adapting to a new norm post-lockdown and a wide range of challenges ahead. When the government made an announcement to provide a stimulus plan to assist those who have been affected due to the pandemic, and only if they were eligible for several stimulus packages, the benefits appeared to be a transitory lifeline for many. Therefore, this chapter presents challenges experienced by the restaurant operators during the COVID-19 pandemic crisis and how the loan moratorium policy has impacted their businesses. This study applies the crisis management theory to understand how the restaurant operators cope with challenges encountered during the volatile and uncertain situation of the COVID-19 pandemic.

The COVID-19 pandemic has caused an unprecedented crisis along the food supply chain and continues to cripple the market which has modified the business landscape vigorously. The restriction of people's movement and the government's call for staying at home has resulted in thousands of food businesses ceasing operations. Businesses were struggling to stay afloat with their overhead expenses and earning significantly less than usual. This situation had led to an inevitable mass retrenchment of employees, particularly in the food service sector. For this reason, the industries have called for government assistance to ease them up during this pandemic crisis, including tax reduction, lower levy for work permit holders, short-term financing without collateral, employee retention scheme, wage subsidy programme, employee retraining programmes, and loan repayment moratorium.

6.1.1 *Crisis management theory*

This study uses crisis management theory in framing the scope of research. The crisis management theory was first introduced from disaster management studies in the 1960s. This theory has become more complex over time, and its application has crossed many disciplines and business subjects. Due to recent developments in the COVID-19 pandemic crisis, few studies were conducted to understand how the businesses deal with the challenges emerging from the pandemic, particularly in the restaurant business. Business owners switched their firm strategies in an effort to sustain and found new opportunities during the pandemic crisis (Kuckertz et al., 2020). Multi firms with different business concepts have survived the COVID-19 crisis by implementing drastic contingency plans through their risk management and financial restructuring (Alves et al., 2020). Business-to-business firms have adapted to risk-mitigating strategies relating to cash flows in their marketing game plans during pandemics (Kang et al., 2020). Basically, under this crisis management theory, three key events must occur: (i) the identification of crisis, (ii) the adaption of contingency strategies, and (iii) the planning of post-crisis measures. This current study focuses on the contingency strategies adapted by the restaurant owners to keep their business operating by understanding the challenges identified and how the loan moratorium policy has impacted their business during the pandemic crisis.

6.1.2 *Loan moratorium policy*

Around the world, many governments have passed billions of dollars as a stimulus package to boost their economies which have been severely

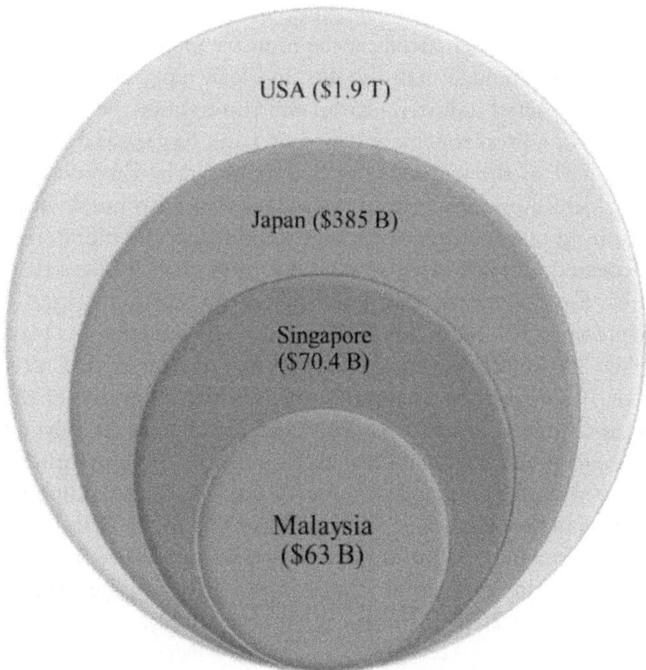

Figure 6.2 Stimulus deals due to COVID-19 across countries

affected by the pandemic crisis (see Figure 6.2). Figure 6.2 illustrates a brief comparison of four economies on how much the stimulus package has been mandated by their governments: the United States has passed nearly $2 trillion of economic stimulus so far; Japan has declared a $385 billion stimulus deal to buffer the COVID-19 impact; Singapore has announced more than $70 billion to mitigate the pandemic impact, and; Malaysia has approved more than $63 billion stimulus package to various sectors that have been hard hit by the crisis. Under the umbrella term 'policy', the stimulus package offers some measures to stimulate the dreadful economy impacted due to the pandemic crisis. In this pandemic context, the economic recovery policy is for a specific term which is normally between three to six months. The policy, somehow, has a long-term effect on the stakeholders. The policy is also subject to changes from time to time, depending on the economic landscape at the time of its introduction and implementation. In most situations, the policy serves as a guideline for the government or organisation to observe in implementing certain measures.

The stimulus package comes in numerous taxation and spending proportions to a broad range of industries. It could exist in the forms of tax reduction, cash aid, grants, moratorium, just to name a few. In efforts to ease the financial burden faced by the industry players, the Government of Malaysia has extended cash payouts and loan repayment moratoriums to help the impacted industries to survive throughout the uncertain circumstances. In a press statement issued by Bank Negara Malaysia (BNM) (2020), as part of the stimulus policy announced by the government, a loan repayment moratorium was imposed on all performing loans. Under the first round of the stimulus package announced, the moratorium policy has covered all loans with arrears, not more than 90 days that could be eligible for a 6-month repayment deferment starting April 1, 2020, until September 30, 2020. The second round of the stimulus plan, after September 30, 2020, was targeted repayment assistance that served the borrowers based on their financial needs. On the other side of the coin, any accrued interest resulted from the deferment must be borne by the borrowers. It should be noted that this loan repayment moratorium served as a blanket stimulus policy to all impacted individuals and industries, with no exception to the restaurant industry. According to the 20th LAKSANA report, approximately 732,000 borrowers who benefitted from the loan moratorium in the first-round stimulus plan have resumed their repayments as of August 2020 (Ministry of Finance, 2020).

6.1.3 Restaurant ownership

Legally speaking, type restaurant ownership is divided into four categories: namely, (i) sole proprietorship, (ii) partnership, (iii) limited liability partnership, and (iv) corporation (which could be registered under private limited or limited entity). Each ownership holds its legal responsibilities, duties, and liabilities and has a different organisational structure that determines how the business affairs are managed for the short- and long-term. While independently-owned ownership could be of any category, but commonly operates with one single outlet. In Malaysia, all restaurant businesses must be registered in compliance with the existing regulations, including, but is not limited to, the Companies Act 2016, the Registrations of Businesses Act 2016, and the Limited Liability Partnership Regulations 2012. Relating to its organisational structure, an independently-owned restaurant could make business decisions in no time and without unnecessary delay compared to restaurants under franchising or licensing structures. Importantly, most independently-owned restaurants have limited cash flows which hamper them from surviving from the crisis impact. Due to that aggravating financial situation, they are left with relatively limited options to stay afloat. For the purpose of this study, only independently-owned restaurant operators were selected and recruited as respondents. The rationale for selecting them as respondents is because the short timeline of the study requires prompt decisions from potential respondents to participate in the data collection process.

This chapter provides a significant contribution to the restaurant industry in facing business challenges, particularly during the pandemic crisis. The inputs shared by the restaurant players on how the moratorium policy provided by the government has impacted their businesses are crucial for the policymakers to provide more effective stimulus plans in the future.

6.2 Method

Malaysia has experienced two rounds of MCO in an effort to flatten the infection curve of COVID-19. The first-round order was executed on March 12, 2020, for a two-week closedown. A series of orders were implemented throughout Malaysia, depending on the infection rates of the districts or states. The second-round order was announced on January 13, 2021. A timeline of first-round orders enforced in Malaysia has illustrated in Figure 6.1. The data collection process of this study adhered to the SOP outlined by the government. In observing the SOP, all interviews were done fully online via Google Meet. This study was conducted during the first round of MCO. A five-step data collection process was completed within a one-month duration (see Figure 6.3). A sequence of interviews via Google Meet was employed among a group of six restaurant owners in Klang Valley.

6.2.1 Identify the population of the study

The first step of this data collection process was identifying the population of the study. There are hundreds of restaurants operating in Klang Valley before the COVID-19 pandemic. These establishments, however, were among the most hit during the first phase of MCO. Due to the closure of

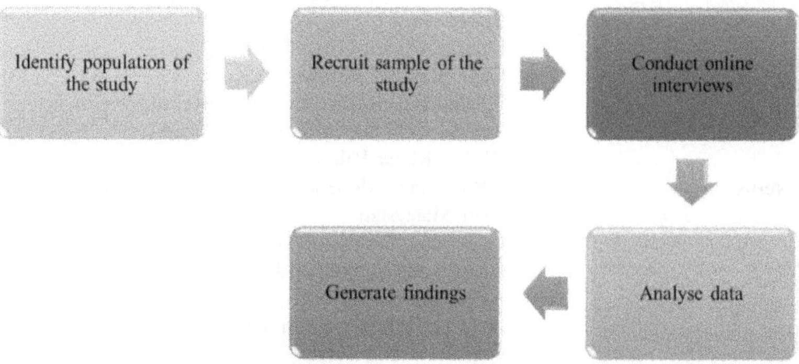

Figure 6.3 Flowchart of the data collection process

many restaurants in Klang Valley, it was a challenge to administer a large number of survey questionnaires. Therefore, a qualitative approach was used for the data collection process.

6.2.2 Recruit sample of the study

For this study, only independently-owned restaurants were selected to get recruited as respondents. The rationale of this sample selection is that the independent restaurant operators could be able to make a faster business decision compared to franchised and multi-branched restaurants. During the recruitment process, potential respondents were contacted through their contact numbers available on their business social media profiles such as Facebook and Instagram. The respondents should have met all the inclusion and exclusion criteria defined for this study. The inclusion and exclusion criteria of the respondents are presented in Table 6.1. Once the respondents agreed to participate in the interviews voluntarily and anonymously, they were asked to sign consent forms. The consent forms were sent to all respondents, and respondents should have returned the signed forms through emails before the interview meeting. All respondents signed the consent forms with their digital signatures. Then, they were given a set of time slots to choose from, based on their preferred time, for attending the interviews through Google Meet.

The interview instrument was developed in reference to crisis management theory with some modifications to provide answers to the research questions. An evaluation of experts was performed to ensure the interview instrument was effective before the real interview took place. A semi-structured open-ended interview was used to allow more in-depth information gathered from

Table 6.1 Inclusion and exclusion criteria of respondents

Inclusion	Independently-owned restaurant Malaysian Operating more than 5 years Still operating during pandemic Having business loan with registered local banks Taking COVID-19 loan moratorium Within Klang Valley
Exclusion	Other than independently-owned restaurants Non-Malaysian Operating less than 5 years Closed during the pandemic No business loan No COVID-19 loan moratorium Outside Klang Valley

the respondents during the interviews. The instrument was divided into three major sections: namely, (i) demographic of the respondents and background of loan type, (ii) experiences in managing financial crisis during COVID-19 pandemic, and (iii) opinions on perceived benefits gained from the moratorium.

6.2.3 *Conduct online interviews*

The next step of the data collection process was conducting the interviews among the respondents. Initially, a total of 12 respondents have agreed to participate in the interview sessions. Eventually, only six participants managed to complete the entire interview. Several attempts were made to accommodate the interview slots time for the rest of the potential respondents. Among the barriers pointed out for conducting the online interviews were the respondents' personal matters, respondents' withdrawal due to emergency cases, respondents' unstable internet connection, and faulty devices. For successful interviews, each session lasted approximately 45 minutes to one hour. The interview sessions were conducted in English as all participants were comfortable conversing in English. All interview sessions were completed within two-week. For a backup, the only audio recording was done as all respondents were not consented to have the sessions recorded. The data saturation point happened after the 6th participant's session as well, and the interviewing process was concluded. For each interview, after the transcription was finalised, data were undergone participant-checking procedures. This procedure was taken to ensure no important data was missing or left out.

6.2.4 *Analyse data*

For data analysis, descriptive statistical analysis was used to analyse the demographic section only. Further, thematic coding was used to generate meaningful findings from the other two sections: experiences and opinions of perceived benefits. At the beginning stage of thematic analysis, transcription was done manually from the audio recordings. Each respondent was assigned with an identifier, for example, ID#01, for a convenient reference.

6.2.5 *Generate findings*

Next, audio recording transcribes were arranged in categories and themes based on the excerpts or keywords patterns that emerged from the data gathered. In the final step, findings were generated in two primary categories: descriptive statistics and thematic statements.

Table 6.2 Descriptive statistics on respondents' demographic, business background, and loan facility

ID	*Types of restaurant*	*Current no. of employees*	*Years in business*	*Information of loan facility*
ID#01	Casual dining	2	6	Still serving one loan facility
ID#02	Casual dining	2	10	Still serving one loan facility
ID#03	Casual dining	4	12	Still serving one loan facility
ID#04	Buffet dining	3	8	Still serving two loan facilities
ID#05	Casual dining	2	10	Still serving two loan facilities
ID#06	Casual dining	8	15	Still serving one loan facility

6.3 Findings

The findings in this study are presented in two categories: (i) descriptive statistics and (ii) interview excerpts and themes. In the first category, descriptive data provides a summary of characteristics of demographics, business background, and information of loan facilities served by the respondents (see Table 6.2).

6.3.1 Descriptive statistics

Of the six respondents, two of them have been in the restaurant business for less than 10 years, and the rest have been in the business for more than 10 years. It showed that they have vast experience in manning the restaurant business and still surviving the pandemic as they were still operating when this interview took place. Nearly all restaurants are operating as casual dining, except one restaurant serves buffet-style dining. The numbers of employees retained are between 2 and 8 people. Only two of them have two loan facilities, while others serve one facility only. All of them took out loan facilities from local financial institutions.

6.3.2 Interview excerpts and themes

The first research question was 'What were your experiences in managing the financial crisis during the COVID-19 pandemic?'. All interview excerpts were tabulated in Table 6.3. From the excerpts, most

Table 6.3 Interview excerpts for research question on 'What were your experiences in managing the financial crisis during COVID-19 pandemic?'

ID	*Excerpts*	*Themes*
ID#01	First round of MCO was very painful. For one week, almost zero customers. I have rental due in 3-week time. I changed my business hours … normally I open for lunch hours only because I have to follow SOP, I open for breakfast and lunch. Very bad sales for take-away because people don't want to go out. I have to terminate my servers … It was a tough decision, but I promised to hire them back if the situation improves. My cash flow dried up within weeks.	• bad experience • bad sales • staff termination • limited cash flows • change business hours • switch to take-away and food delivery
ID#02	This COVID-19 is a nightmare for any business. I never expect this pandemic can be so disastrous to small businesses like me. The first week of MCO, I was shocked … no customers dine-in so the sales dropped tremendously. I get scared because I have to pay rental & my workers' salaries very soon. I can say my sales dropped likes 90%, and I still open shop for take-away. Take-away was not so good too. You can see all regular customers disappear for weeks because everyone stops travelling & socialising. I reduced my business expenses by giving daily salary to my staff … some left voluntarily because I was not able to pay them like in the past. Business was very challenging.	• bad experience • bad sales • staff quit • limited cash flows • reduce overhead • daily basis pays • switch to take-away
ID#03	My restaurant serves hot cooking only and open from 5 pm to 2 am before COVID-19. When everyone must stay home & the SOP for business was that the business hour must open during day time only with no dine-in, I lost my earning nearly 100% for a couple of days. Then, I decided to open day time with the same menu … it was tough because my regular customers did not turn in at this hour. I have to terminate some of my workers … more than half of 12 workers … SOP compliance requires only 30% staff on-premise. I retained 4 workers only, and I myself did some deliveries and kitchen works. I paid their salary on a daily basis, but the earning was very little compared to prior to the pandemic. I have to borrow from my parents to cover my business expenses.	• bad experience • bad sales • staff termination • reduce overhead • change business hours • borrow from parents • switch to take-away and food delivery

(Continued)

Table 6.3 (*Continued*)

ID	*Excerpts*	*Themes*
ID#04	Before the COVID-19 hit our country, my restaurant was very packed during breakfast and lunchtime. Every day my restaurant almost full house with customers dining-in and some catering services for functions. Come COVID … everything got crashed … no customers and no income … In a month, I reduced my menu from 70 plus to just 20 plus because the overhead was so high and it did not match the sales. Even catering bookings were all cancelled. Worse, customers asked for refund which I paid because I need to maintain my good reputation. I asked for rental discount from my landlord and luckily, he understands my situation. I have been renting his shop for more than 5 years, so I got 50% off for my monthly rental for 3 months. I also sold some of my equipment and furniture because I need cash badly to pay my workers. I usually pay them in a fortnight, but since the pandemic, I pay them on daily basis. I used to have 10 workers but now only 3 are still working with me. Now, my restaurant just does take-away, and we partnered up with some delivery companies for food delivery.	• bad experience • bad sales • staff termination • reduce overhead • smaller menu list • reduced rental • switch to take-away and food delivery
ID#05	In fact, I closed my restaurant for the first week of MCO because I got confused over the SOP. Then, when I got a clearer picture about the SOP, then I re-opened the business, but I lost my regular customers. Before COVID, dine-in was common and I don't really do delivery because I don't have the manpower to handle it. As this business is manned by myself, my spouse and two workers, our overhead is not that high. It just I need to commit for my rental & salary for my staff. I didn't get any discount for my rental, but the landlord was kind enough to waive my first-month rental during MCO … only for March 2020. Because operating hour was very short, I focus on delivery only. My spouse helped me with the delivery as well, even though I used delivery riders. But sales dropped about 70–80% because people cook at home, and many home-based businesses suddenly emerged.	• bad experience • bad sales • reduce overhead • waived one-month rental • switch to food delivery

ID#06	Never thought of this crisis before and how pandemic can cause terrible situation to our economy. Slowdown in business is pretty normal, but this pandemic is something that you never imagined can happen in the next 100 years. Before the pandemic, my business uses food delivery and social media for sales & customer engagement but not so active as the majority of customers still love to dine in, and some do take-away. Due to business hour restriction and customers were forced to stay home, I increase the social media marketing and sign up for several delivery services so I could still make some money. I may say … my sales dropped to about 70% in the first & second month and until now is not fully recovered like usual. I own the shop and no bank commitment for this property so really have no worry about the rental at all. I managed to retain all my staff … just delegate new task like delivery, take-away counter and web management. But their pay doesn't remain the same, I offer them daily basis salary with no benefits. I use my own saving to cover some business expenses as well. Some supplies become quite expensive like fresh produce, so the profit is affected too. You cannot increase the price because customers will turn away.	• bad experience • bad sales • low overhead (daily pay with no benefit) • limited cash flows • change business hours • switch to food delivery

respondents acknowledged that the COVID-19 pandemic was a bad experience for business and sales have been severely affected, between 60% to nearly 100%. In coping with the crisis, all respondents tried to reduce their overhead expenses by changing business hours in compliance with the SOP, downsizing the staffing, replacing monthly salary to daily pay (without benefits) for the staff, reducing numbers of menus served, manning the business themselves, and switching to a new norm of selling food - take-away and food delivery. Some respondents managed to have reduced their premises rental, while only one owned the shop premise with no loan facility. Due to limited cash

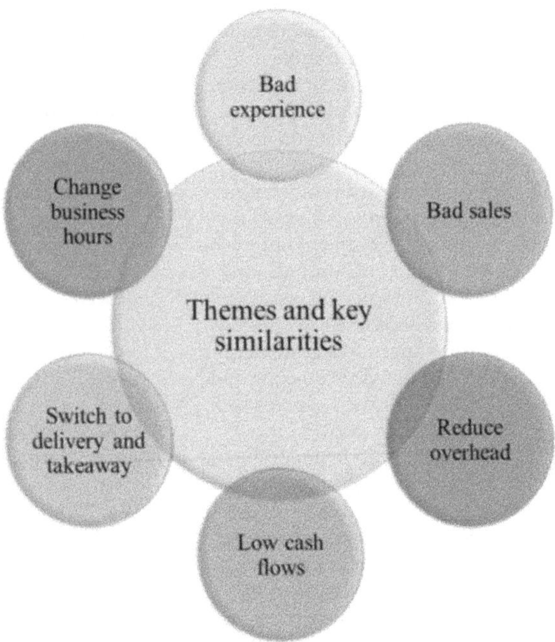

Figure 6.4 Themes and key similarities in restaurant operators' experiences on impact of COVID-19 crisis to their businesses

flows, most respondents used their savings or borrowed from their parents, to sustain their business. In brief, the themes are summarised in Figure 6.4 for easy reference.

The second research question was 'What are your opinions on the perceived benefits gained from the moratorium?'. All interview excerpts were categorised in Table 6.4. From the excerpts, one major theme emerged to label the moratorium: short-term benefit. All respondents agreed that the moratorium offered them a short-term benefit (six months) while their businesses were still in survival mode beyond the moratorium period. Some respondents thought that the interest-free moratorium should be offered and its application must be hassle-free. They agreed that the application was time-consuming. The respondents also suggested that terms and conditions for other financial aid, that is wage subsidy, should be friendly to the businesses during this pandemic. The key similarities of the themes are summarised in Figure 6.5 for easy reference.

Table 6.4 Interview excerpts for research question on 'What are your opinions on the perceived benefits gained from the moratorium?'

ID	*Excerpts*	*Themes*
ID#01	I think the moratorium is just to show that government cares for those who are affected by the pandemic. Six-month deferment is not enough actually for the recovery. As you can see, people are not spending like before, so the business still needs time to recover. One thing for sure because the business is never be the same as before the pandemic. The second round of the moratorium is another headache. The government should impose an automatic moratorium instead of targeted assistance because the application and approval are time-consuming.	• short-term benefit • easy application process
ID#02	The idea of the moratorium is for temporarily aid only. But business never returns to normal like before the lockdown. People are still afraid to dine-in and very careful with their expenses. The government should impose an interest-free moratorium and removed all conditions attached to the moratorium.	• short-term benefit • interest-free moratorium • easy application process
ID#03	The moratorium should be extended for those who have less than 60% of income or sales. When my moratorium was approved, my rental was about dues and sales were very bad, I have to borrow from my parents to pay my business expenses. I think apart from the moratorium, government should offer short-term loans without collateral to allow businesses to have more cash flows.	• short-term benefit • easy application process • other financial aid
ID#04	The 6-month moratorium was good but not good enough to allow my business to heal from the impact. I need more time, but the policy is not helping … The moratorium should be interest-free and the extension (second-round) should be automatic as well. But for those who wanted to resume their repayment can do so right away.	• short-term benefit • interest-free moratorium • easy application process
ID#05	In my opinion, the loan moratorium is helping my business just fine. Frankly speaking, after six-month moratorium, my business was not making much profit and I am not sure if the (moratorium) extension will help me because people are not spending like usual. If I extend the moratorium, I will need to pay interest accrued from the moratorium. So, it's not helping me to reduce my expenses or monthly commitments. Business is still struggling as limited dine-in SOP and food become more expensive if you use delivery services. The policymakers should do a survey to get business operators' opinions.	• short-term benefit • interest-free moratorium

(Continued)

Table 6.4 (Continued)

ID	*Excerpts*	*Themes*
ID#06	I took the first-round moratorium when I started to fork out my own savings. The moratorium should come in line with another stimulus, I should say. For example, the wage subsidy is good, but the conditions for eligibility are not pretty. The government should have listened to the stakeholders' opinions (not only banks) before implementing the second-round moratorium.	• short-term benefit • other financial aid • tight eligibility for subsidy

6.4 Conclusion

COVID-19 pandemic has caused a catastrophic effect on many economies, with no exception to the restaurant industry. This study extends its contribution in both theoretical and practical implications, particularly for the restaurant business and their crisis management strategy during the COVID-19 pandemic.

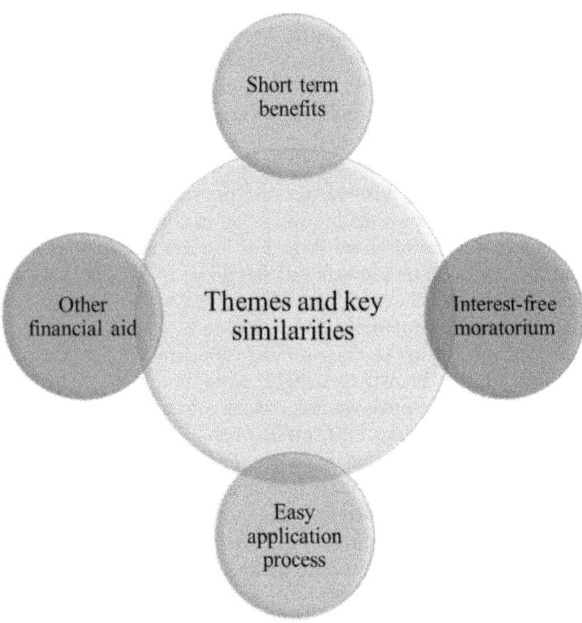

Figure 6.5 Themes and key similarities in restaurant operators' opinions relating to loan moratorium policy

6.4.1 Implications of the study

The findings generated from this study provides addition of new information to the existing literature for the restaurant industry, particularly in dealing with an excruciating crisis like the COVID-19 pandemic. In dealing with a crisis, contingency strategies are crucial to ensure the business remains viable. In general, independently-owned businesses with limited cash flows reduced their expenses by downsizing the operation in many ways, depending on their own needs, and adapting to a new norm or SOP implemented by the government. Practically, findings from this study recommend that the policymakers must consider the opinion and suggestions from the restaurant industry as they are the ones most impacted during the crisis.

6.4.2 Limitations and recommendations

This study has acknowledged some limitations and therefore, some recommendations are proposed for future research. Those limitations include a short timeline for the entire study, restricted location for sampling size, the unreliable online platform for interviewing purposes, and single selection of business ownership. First of all, the study was launched during the early weeks of the first-round of MCO and completed before the MCO ended. This short timeline has led to a qualitative approach and the employment of interviews of six respondents only as a longer time was needed to recruit more respondents. Due to a small sample size, the inputs gathered were not satisfactorily adequate for generalisation. A future study could explore the administration of survey questionnaires to provide a generalisation of the food service industry. Next, the recruited respondents were chosen from Klang Valley only. This recruitment was closely related to this self-funded study where it has a limited spending budget on honorarium for the respondents. Therefore, the data collected was not representative of the food service sector in Malaysia. Future research should consider reaching for restaurant operators in other states and federal territories if there is a sufficient fund to invite participants.

Due to the COVID-19 pandemic and the need for SOP observation, an online platform was the best option available to conduct interviews in this study. The drawback in using the online platform for data collection was the faulty devices and instability of internet connection. It is recommended that face-to-face interviews could be done in the future study to obtain more trustworthy data from the respondents if the situation permits. This current study also focused on a single type of restaurant ownership, that is independently-owned restaurants. Future research might seek other types of restaurant ownership such as partnership-owned restaurants or franchised restaurants for more intriguing and useful data which could be used as a reference by the policymakers and other stakeholders in the business decision-making process, especially while experiencing a crisis.

Acknowledgement

The author received no financial support for the research, authorship, and publication of this chapter.

Summary

- The loan moratorium policy has a minor impact on the restaurant industry in helping them to sustain during the pandemic.
- The policymakers should take into account the restaurant operators' opinions before implementing the loan moratorium policy.
- The loan moratorium policy should incorporate other stimulus packages to provide better assistance to the restaurant operators.

References

Alves, J. C., Lok, T. C., Luo, Y., & Hao, W. (2020). Crisis challenges of small firms in Macao during the COVID-19 pandemic. *Frontiers of Business Research in China*, *14*(1), 1–23.

Azman, N. H. (2020, April 29). Mamak restaurants ponder business under new normal. *The Malaysian Reserve*. https://themalaysianreserve.com/2020/04/29/mamak-restaurants-ponder-business-under-new-normal/

Bank Negara Malaysia (2020). Measures to assist individuals, SMEs and corporates affected by COVID-19. https://www.bnm.gov.my/-/measures-to-assist-individuals-smes-and-corporates-affected-by-covid-19

Kang, J., Diao, Z., & Zanini, M. T. (2020). Business-to-business marketing responses to COVID-19 crisis: a business process perspective. In *Marketing Intelligence and Planning*. https://doi.org/10.1108/MIP-05-2020-0217

Kuckertz, A., Brändle, L., Gaudig, A., Hinderer, S., Reyes, C. A. M., Prochotta, A., & Berger, E. S. (2020). Startups in times of crisis–A rapid response to the COVID-19 pandemic. *Journal of Business Venturing Insights*, *13*. https://doi.org/10.1016/j.jbvi.2020.e00169

Malay Mail (2020, April 15). Data expert shares tips empower SMEs surviving MCO. *Bernama*. https://www.malaymail.com/news/money/2020/04/15/data-expert-shares-tips-to-empower-smes-in-surviving-mco/1856966

Ministry of Finance (2020). Media statement: Implementation of the Prihatin Rakyat Economic Stimulus Package (PRIHATIN) and National Economic Recovery Plan (PENJANA). https://pre2020.treasury.gov.my/pdf/Speech-20th-Laksana-Report-Implementation-Of-PRIHATIN.pdf

7 The impact of COVID-19 on tourism in Malaysia

Insights from domestic tourists' travel intentions

Jingyi Li, Fumitaka Furuoka, Beatrice Lim, and Khairul Hanim Pazim

7.1 Introduction

7.1.1 Background

In modern society, travel is a crucial economic activity, and, at the same time, it is considered a fundamental human need (Bae & Chang, 2021; Ding et al., 2020). Due to the spread of the COVID-19 pandemic, 100% of all worldwide destinations and more than 200 countries have been affected (UNWTO, 2020). The unprecedented measures that have been implemented by governments worldwide (e.g., travel ban and physical distance) have brought the tourism economy to a standstill (OCDE, 2020). Approximately 96% of the overall world population has been affected by international travel bans (Neuburger & Egger, 2021). The World Tourism Organization (UNWTO) has forecasted a vast loss of at least 22 billion dollars (Zhu & Deng, 2020). The tourism industry has profoundly impacted and faced an unprecedented challenge in modern times with the outbreak of COVID-19 in 2020 (Williams, 2020).

Before the outbreak of the COVID-19 pandemic, humans have suffered from several health crises such as Spanish influenza, SARS, MERS, Ebola, swine flu, Zika, and yellow fever (Aydın & Ari, 2020). COVID-19 is a far more significant threat to the global tourism market and travel behaviour than the previous pandemic outbreaks (e.g., SARS, H1N1, or Ebola) (Wen et al., 2020; Zhu & Deng, 2020). Besides, it is worth noting that the COVID-19 pandemic has fundamentally changed the world by affecting people's lives and lifestyles (Accenture, 2020). Consumers' confidence and behaviour have been affected by the COVID-19 pandemic and travel restrictions (OCDE, 2020). For example, over 50% of consumers are unwilling to travel or choose a hotel to stay in during the COVID-19 pandemic (Gursoy & Chi, 2020). Moreover, with a greater understanding of travellers' safety, health threats can significantly affect their travel

DOI: 10.4324/9781003182740-7

decision-making (Huang et al., 2020). When a tourist suffers from risks during a trip, it can bring tourists and tourism practitioners problems (Bae & Chang, 2021). Thus, there is a conflicting need for travelling and safety (Bae & Chang, 2021; Ding et al., 2020).

As a result, the tourism industry and practitioners need to reconsider the tourism market and understand the changes in people's attitudes and behaviour towards tourism during the COVID-19 pandemic. In past research, numerous studies have examined the tourists' risk perception in the aftermath of health crises (e.g., SARS, H1N1, or Ebola) (Neuburger & Egger, 2021). However, previous studies lack the knowledge about COVID-19, which is a far more significant threat to the global tourism market and travel behaviour (Wen et al., 2020; Zhu & Deng, 2020) than the impact of former tourism crises on tourists' risk perception and travel intentions (Neuburger & Egger, 2021). In conclusion, there is a need to find more evidence to help the tourism industry and practitioners to understand tourist's travel intentions.

7.1.2 Theory of planned behaviour

According to Ajzen and Kruglanski (2019), the theory of planned behaviour as one of the most common psychological models has been applied to predict, understand and explain a wide variety of individual actions by identifying the individual's intentions in social science research. Three antecedents jointly determine such intentions, attitude, norms, and behavioural control, affecting behaviour (Bae & Chang, 2021; Boguszewicz-Kreft et al., 2020; Chaulagain et al., 2021). Attitude is defined as the degree to which an individual positively or negatively assesses behaviour and is assumed to be based on accessible behavioural beliefs (Ajzen & Kruglanski, 2019). Subjective norm is defined as an individual's perception of how the most important others to him or her would think of the behaviour and is based on accessible normative beliefs (Ajzen & Kruglanski, 2019; Chaulagain et al., 2021). Perceived behavioural control is known to be perceived capability or inability to execute behaviour and is believed to be based on accessible control beliefs (Ajzen & Kruglanski, 2019). Behavioural intentions emphasise one's intent to travel or a commitment to travel, and it is an outcome of a mental process that leads to action into behaviour (Ajzen & Kruglanski, 2019). In short, the theory of planned behaviour examines that behavioural intentions are significant when the individual's attitude to the behaviour is positive; when individuals are encouraged by the people who are essential to them and believe they have the capabilities to practice the behaviour (Callow et al., 2020). Thus, in line with previous research, this study applies the theory of planned behaviour as one of the theoretical frameworks.

7.1.3 Risk perception and travel

The theory of risk perception proposed originally by Bauer in 1960, which is an essential theoretical basis, explains consumers' decision-making behaviour (Wang et al., 2020). In other words, individuals will reduce their risk actions when taking a risk-related problem (Waters et al., 2019). Travel risk perception is the tourists' judgment of the uncertain activities or processes in tourism, impacting tourists' decision-making behaviours if they believe the perceived risk is beyond acceptance (Wang et al., 2020). Individuals generally rate the likelihood of future events using the available heuristics; therefore, the researchers usually have tested the risk perception instead of real risk due to individuals' risk perception as the primary determinant of human behaviour (Bae and Chang, 2021).

Based on previous studies, tourism scholars have discussed at length the relationship between perceived risk and tourism behaviours since the 1990s, and risk perception has been shown to play an essential role in individual travel decision-making (Huang et al., 2020). In this study, COVID-19 is categorised under the health risk that impacts the individuals' decision behaviours in tourism. Moreover, the health risk (e.g., SARS, H1N1, and Ebola) has been proven to impact the tourism economy and tourist travel intentions (Neuburger & Egger, 2021). In terms of the unprecedented COVID-19 pandemic, it is necessary to explain the relationship between the risk perception of COVID-19 and travel intentions. Some researchers have reported that potential tourists' travel intentions have changed due to the outbreak of the COVID-19 pandemic (Wang et al., 2020).

This study employs the extended theory of planned behaviour to explain the relationship of travel intentions to Malaysia's domestic tourism by adding the risk perception as an antecedent during the COVID-19 pandemic. In the context of Malaysian tourism, based on the survey on domestic travel in Malaysia (Tourism Malaysia, 2020), the findings present that most of the respondents choose domestic tourism over international tourism due to the effects of COVID-19 on their attitude towards travelling. According to existing studies, risk perception was added into the theory of planned behaviour as a successful model to be tested in tourism. For example, the theory of planned behaviour was used to predict tourists' health-related behaviour and travelling satisfaction towards Tibet (Huang et al., 2020).

7.1.4 Gender and travel behaviour

As a classical framework describing people's decision-making process, the Theory of Planned Behaviour has been widely applied and enriched over the past few decades (Liu et al., 2020). For example, according to (Ajzen

& Kruglanski, 2019), the paper has been extending the model by adding background factors such as age, gender, education, personality, emotions, and knowledge. Karl et al. (2020) also states that gender difference is found between actual and intentional behaviour. Their research presents that the probability of planning a trip in the following year is lower for females compared to male tourists (Karl et al., 2020). Moreover, one study shows a significant moderating effect by gender in the relationship between affective risk perception and behavioural intention (Bae & Chang, 2021). Although studies confirm that the gender of tourists affects their tourism behaviour (Boguszewicz-Kreft et al., 2020), there is little research studied in the context of COVID-19 and the travel intentions.

Therefore, this study attempts to explain the differences in the domestic travel intentions and its predictors before and during the COVID-19 pandemic. This study hypothesises that there are differences between male and female respondents based on the relationships among risk perception, attitude, subjective norm, perceived behavioural control, and travel intentions. Therefore, to examine travel risk perception and travel intentions during the COVID-19 pandemic, research hypotheses could be formulated as follow:

Hypothesis 1: Risk perception would affect attitude, subjective norms, perceived control behaviour, and travel intentions toward domestic travel during the COVID-19 pandemic.

Hypothesis 2: Gender would influence the attitude, subjective norm, perceived control behaviour, and travel intentions toward domestic travel before and during the COVID-19 pandemic.

7.2 Method

7.2.1 Sample

This research leads to a novel perspective on the development of risk perception and travel intentions by comparing the two phases of the before and during the COVID-19 pandemic by collecting and analysing empirical evidence. The survey was conducted using the online Google form and sent directly to 51 potential Malaysian travellers (above 18-years old) from October 2020 to December 2020.

7.2.2 Instrument and measures

The survey instrument was a self-administered questionnaire divided into three sections: demographic information, the theory of planned behaviour, and risk perception. In this study, the first section of the questionnaire involved respondents' demographic information, including gender, age, education level, marital status, and past travelling experience. In the second section of the questionnaire, based on the theory of planned behaviour (Ajzen & Kruglanski, 2019), this analysis considers three elements: attitude, subjective norm, and perceived behavioural control. Thus, this section focuses on the variables related to attitude, the subjective norm, perceived behavioural control, and travel intentions during the COVID-19 pandemic. The last section relates to the risk perception variables.

According to Table 7.4 (see Appendix 1), measurements for the conceptual model have been adapted from previous studies' existing scales (Bae & Chang, 2021; Chaulagain et al., 2021; Lee et al., 2012; Sánchez-Cañizares et al., 2021; Yang et al., 2015). The wording of scale items had been modified to fit the context of travel intentions and risk perception of COVID-19. The modified measurement is shown in Appendix 1 (Table 7.4). All constructs were measured with multiple items on five-point Likert Scales (e.g., 1 = strongly disagree to 5 = strongly agree), except the "Risk perception 1" which would be measured with (1 = not at all worried to 5 = very worried). There were a total of 15 variables for measuring the risk perception (3 variables), tourists' attitude towards domestic travel (3 variables), subjective norm towards domestic travel (3 variables), perceived behavioural control towards domestic travel intentions (3 variables), and travel intentions (3 variables). At the end of 2020, the study collected 51 valid samples. IBM SPSS 24.0 was used to analyse the data.

7.3 Findings

7.3.1 Demographic information

Table 7.1 shows that the overall sample consisted of 34.9% male and 64.7% female respondents in Malaysia. The majority of respondents were within the age range of 18–54 years. Among them, 94.1% of respondents have a Bachelor's degree and above education background, and 84.5% of the respondents are unmarried. According to the past travelling experience in 2019, 11.8% of respondents travelled 0 times, 23.5% of them travelled 1–2 times, "3–4 times" accounted for 29.4%, and 27.4% of respondents travelled 5–6 times and more.

7.3.2 The Difference in the four constructs of theory of planned behaviour (TPB) towards domestic travel before and during the pandemic

Table 7.2 reports the mean values and standard deviations of each of the four constructs before and during the COVID-19 pandemic. As the results have shown, there is a drop in scores for all four constructs during

Table 7.1 Demographic information of potential Malaysian travellers ($n = 51$)

		n	%			*n*	%
Age	18–24	25	49	Gender	Male	17	33.3
	25–34	15	29.4		Female	34	66.7
	35–44	7	13.7	Marital status	Unmarried	43	84.3
	45–54 and above	4	7.8		Married	8	15.7
Education	Doctorate degree	3	5.9	Past travelling experiences in 2019	0 time	6	11.8
	Master's degree	13	25.5		1–2 times	12	23.5
	Bachelor's degree	32	62.7		3–4 times	15	29.4
	Diploma	1	2		5–6 times	9	17.6
	Secondary school	2	3.9		7–10 times	3	5.9
	Primary school and others	3	5.9		11–15 times	2	3.9
					16 times and more	4	7.8

the pandemic. The findings indicate a drop in the belief and changes in travel intentions toward domestic travel during the COVID-19 pandemic. The mean scores of the attitude moderately decrease from 3.634 to 2.673. By contrast, there is a radical decrease in the mean scores of perceived behavioural control, from 4.359 to 2.198. The mean score of subjective norm also declined from 4.189 to 2.281.

Similarly, the mean scores of domestic travel intentions declined from 4.222 to 2.375. In other words, the COVID-19 pandemic has a significant negative effect on Malaysians' confidence in the capacity (i.e., perceived behavioural control) of domestic travel. Simultaneously, the pandemic also has a moderate negative effect on the Malaysians' favourable evaluation (i.e., attitude) of domestic travel.

Table 7.2 Mean values and standard deviations of attitude, subjective norm, perceived behavioural control, and domestic travel intentions

	Pre-COVID-19 pandemic period		*COVID-19 pandemic period*			
	Mean	*Standard deviation*	*Mean*	*Standard deviation*	*Mean difference*	*t-statistics*
Attitude	3.634	0.521	2.673	0.722	0.960	5.120*
Subjective norm	4.189	0.912	2.281	0.907	1.909	9.480*
Perceived behavioural control	4.359	0.714	2.189	0.760	2.169	11.724*
Domestic travel intentions	4.222	0.762	2.375	1.008	1.849	9.125*

*Statistically significant at the 5% level.

On the other hand, the standard deviation of attitude moderately increased from 0.521 to 0.722, and the standard deviation of perceived behavioural control marginal increased from 0.714 to 0.760. It means that the COVID-19 pandemic has a moderate effect on the dispersion of favourable evaluations (i.e., attitude) and the ability (i.e., perceived behavioural control) on domestic travel. By contrast, the standard deviation of domestic travel intentions radically increased from 0.762 to 1.008. It may imply that the pandemic has a severe impact on the dispersion of domestic travel intentions. Malaysian people would have a much broader opinion on motivation (i.e., intentions) on domestic travel during the COVID-19 pandemic. Interestingly, the standard deviation of the subjective norm decreased from 0.912 to 0.907. It will mean that Malaysian citizens could have a narrower set of opinions on their domestic travel expectations.

Table 7.2 indicates the findings from the paired sample t-test to compare the beliefs and intentions between the before and during the COVID-19 pandemic. The paired sample t-test could be used to examine whether there is a statistically significant difference in the mean scores on these four constructs. As the findings indicated, there is a statistically significant mean difference between the two periods. It means that the pandemic has a significant impact on the attitude, subjective norm, perceived behavioural control, and domestic travel intentions. Among the four constructs, perceived behavioural control has the highest mean difference, while attitude has the lowest mean difference. In other words, the pandemic would have the most significant impact on the perceived behavioural control and the least impact on attitude.

7.3.3 Gender difference in the four constructs of TPB towards domestic travel before and during pandemic

Table 7.3 reports the gender difference in the mean scores and standard deviations on four constructs. In the pre-COVID-19 pandemic, female respondents tend to have higher mean scores for all these constructs, except attitude. In other words, female respondents have a higher level of norms, ability (i.e., perceived behavioural control), and motivation (i.e., travel intentions) on domestic travel. In contrast, male respondents have a relatively more favourable evaluation (i.e., attitude) on travel. However, the COVID-19 pandemic seems to have a greater/more significant impact on the female respondent than male respondents. As a consequence of the pandemic, the male respondents have a higher level of attitude, subjective norm, and perceived behavioural control, whereas the female respondent has slightly higher domestic travel intentions.

Table 7.3 Mean scores and standard deviations of gender differences on attitude, subjective norm, perceived behavioural control, and domestic travel intentions before and during the COVID-19 pandemic

	Male					
	Pre-COVID-19 pandemic period		*COVID-19 pandemic period*			
	Mean	*Standard deviation*	*Mean*	*Standard deviation*	*Mean difference*	*t-statistics*
Attitude	3.686	0.516	2.676	0.790	1.009	6.564*
Subjective norm	4.176	0.896	2.343	0.915	1.833	7.607*
Perceived behavioural control	4.294	0.742	2.294	0.718	2.001	10.212*
Domestic travel intentions	4.137	0.791	2.352	0.977	1.784	7.395*
	Female					
	Pre-COVID-19 pandemic period		*COVID-19 pandemic period*			
	Mean	*Standard deviation*	*Mean*	*Standard deviation*	*Mean difference*	*t-statistics*
Attitude	3.529	0.528	2.666	0.565	0.862	4.769*
Subjective norm	4.219	0.971	2.156	0.906	2.058	5.537*
Perceived behavioural control	4.490	0.657	1.980	0.820	2.509	9.003*
Domestic travel intentions	4.392	0.689	2.418	1.096	1.980	5.157*

*Statistically significant at the 5% level.

During the pre-COVID-19 pandemic period, male respondents tend to have a more dispersed opinion on the ability (i.e., perceived behavioural control) and motivation (i.e., domestic travel intentions), and female respondents tend to have a more dispersed opinion on favourable evaluation (i.e., attitude) and norms. However, the pandemics have an impact on the dispersion of all these four constructs. Among the male respondents, the standard deviation for all four constructs, except perceived behavioural control, increased during the COVID-19 pandemic period. By contrast, among the female respondents, the standard deviation of all four constructs, except subjective norm, increased during the pandemic.

Moreover, Table 7.3 demonstrates the paired sample t-test to compare the mean difference between male and female respondents. As shown in the results, there is a statistically significant mean difference in all four constructs: attitude, norms, behavioural control, and travel intentions for both male and female respondents. It indicates that the pandemic of COVID-19 will substantially affect these four constructs for both male and female respondents. In other words, the pandemic will change the beliefs and travel intentions of all respondents on domestic travel, regardless of the gender difference. Notably, female respondents have higher mean differences for all these four constructs, except attitude, than male respondents. In other words, the COVID-19 pandemic has a stronger impact on the female respondents' norms, behavioural control, and travel intentions. Especially, there is a significant gender difference in the ability (i.e., perceived behavioural control). The mean difference in male respondents' ability is 2.001, while the mean difference in female respondents' ability is 2.509. It would mean that the pandemic would have an enormous impact on the perceived level of ability to conduct domestic travel among female respondents.

7.4 Conclusion

This study explores changes in the attitude, subjective norms, perceived behavioural control, and travel intentions between pre-COVID-19 and during COVID-19 among Malaysians and explains the gender difference in the respondents' attitude, subjective norm, and perceived behavioural control and travel intentions toward domestic travel between pre-COVID-19 and during COVID-19. The two hypotheses were tested. Firstly, the empirical findings support Hypothesis 1 on the significant impact of risk perception on attitude, subjective norms, perceived control behaviour, and domestic travel intentions toward domestic travel during the COVID-19 pandemic. Secondly, the findings support Hypothesis 2 on the significant impact of gender on attitude, subjective norms, perceived control behaviour, and domestic travel intentions toward domestic travel during the COVID-19 pandemic.

For theoretical implications, this study uses the theoretical generalizability of TPB to explain risky behaviours such as domestic travel during the pandemic. According to the data collection and data analysis, the findings fill the academic gap by investigating the relationships among individuals' risk perception and travel intentions towards Malaysia's domestic tourism during COVID-19. Thus, this study provides a new reference to predict tourists' travel intentions toward domestic travel during the pandemic for the tourism industry regarding the findings. Moreover, this study gives the tourism industry and practitioners a better understanding of individuals' travel intentions toward domestic travel during the pandemic in Malaysia. Finally, this study contributes to the health crisis in tourism literature, which incorporates the current ongoing issue of COVID-19.

As for the practical implications, this study proposes a new measurement to help the tourism industry and practitioners to observe tourists' behavioural intentions related to the risk perception of COVID-19 in Malaysia and the global tourism market. Besides, as discussed above, COVID-19 has a profound impact on the tourism market and tourists. For the tourism industry, it is necessary to rethink tourists' behaviour and the new norms in tourism. This study provides a theoretical basis for tourism practitioners to design better strategies and implications that could encourage tourists to engage in domestic tourism and support the tourism industry.

The lack of sufficient respondents could be considered as the main shortcoming of the current study. This study also uses two questionnaire items to measure construct because of an insufficient number of observations. In a future study, the researcher may consider to use a larger number of the respondent and to increase the number of items in the questionnaire. These studies would provide valuable insight into the relationship between risk perception and travel intention during the pandemic.

Acknowledgement

This research was supported by the Universiti Malaya COVID-19 related special research grant (Grant No. CSRG014-2020SS).

Summary

- This paper examines the impact of risk perception of the COVID-19 pandemic on domestic travel intention over two different time points, namely the before and during the COVID-19 pandemic in Malaysia.
- This study confirms the effects of the COVID-19 pandemic on the four constructs of TPB toward domestic travel during the COVID-19 pandemic.
- The study indicates that the COVID-19 pandemic has a stronger impact on the female respondents' attitudes, norms, behavioural control, and travel intentions toward domestic travel during the COVID-19 pandemic.
- The findings have some significant policy implications.

References

Accenture (2020). How COVID-19 will permanently change consumer behavior: Fast changing consumer behaviors influence the future of the CPG industry. https://www.accenture.com/_acnmedia/PDF-123/Accenture-COVID19-Pulse-Survey-Research-PoV.pdf

Ajzen, I., & Kruglanski, A. W. (2019). Reasoned action in the service of goal pursuit. *Psychological Review*, *126*(5), 774–786. https://doi.org/10.1037/rev0000155

Aydın, L., & Ari, I. (2020). The impact of Covid-19 on Turkey55goal pursuitenture-COVID19-Pulse-Survey-Research-PoV.pdfourists' risk perception of risky destinations: The case of Sab. *Energy Exploration & Exploitation*, 014459872093400. https://doi.org/10.1177/0144598720934007

Bae, S. Y., & Chang, P.-J. (2021). The effect of coronavirus disease-19 (COVID-19) risk perception on behavioural intention towards ' risk perception of risky destinaring the first wave of the pandemic (March 2020). *Current Issues in Tourism*, 24(7), 1–19. https://doi.org/10.1080/13683500.2020.1798895

Boguszewicz-Kreft, M., Kuczamer-Kłopotowska, S., Kozłowski, A., Ayci, A., & Abuhashesh, M. (2020). The theory of planned behaviour in medical tourism: International comparison in the young consumer segment. *International Journal of Environmental Research and Public Health*, *17*(5), 1–17. https://doi.org/10.3390/ijerph17051626

Callow, M. A., Callow, D. D., & Smith, C. (2020). Older adults' intention to socially isolate once COVID-19 stay-at-home orders are replaced with "safer-at-home" public health advisories: A survey of respondents in Maryland. *Journal of Applied Gerontology*, 39(11), 1175–1183. https://doi.org/10.1177/0733464820944704

Chaulagain, S., Pizam, A., & Wang, Y. (2021). An integrated behavioral model for medical tourism: An American perspective. *Journal of Travel Research*, *60*(4), 761-778. https://doi.org/10.1177/0047287520907681

Ding, Y., Xu, J., Huang, S., Li, P., Lu, C., & Xie, S. (2020). Risk perception and depression in public health crises: Evidence from the Covid-19 crisis in China. *International Journal of Environmental Research and Public Health*, *17*(16), 1–17. https://doi.org/10.3390/ijerph17165728

Gursoy, D., & Chi, C. G. (2020). Effects of COVID-19 pandemic on hospitality industry: Review of the current situations and a research agenda. *Journal of Hospitality Marketing and Management*, *29*(5), 527–529. https://doi.org/10.1080/19368623.2020.1788231

Huang, X., Dai, S., & Xu, H. (2020). Predicting tourists' health risk preventative behaviour and travelling satisfaction in Tibet: Combining the theory of planned behaviour and health belief model. *Tourism Management Perspectives*, *33*(January 2020), 100589. https://doi.org/10.1016/j.tmp.2019.100589

Karl, M., Bauer, A., Ritchie, W. B., & Passauer, M. (2020). The impact of travel constraints on travel decision-making: A comparative approach of travel frequencies and intended travel participation. *Journal of Destination Marketing and Management*, *18*(September), 100471. https://doi.org/10.1016/j.jdmm.2020.100471

Lee, C., Song, H., Bendle, L. J., Kim, M., & Han, H. (2012). The impact of non-pharmaceutical interventions for 2009 H1N1 influenza on travel intentions: A model of goal-directed behavior. *Tourism Management*, *33*(1), 89–99. https://doi.org/10.1016/j.tourman.2011.02.006

Liu, A., Ma, E., Qu, H., & Ryan, B. (2020). Daily green behavior as an antecedent and a moderator for visitors' pro-environmental behaviors. *Journal of Sustainable Tourism*, *28*(9), 1390–1408. https://doi.org/10.1080/09669582.2020.1741598

Neuburger, L., & Egger, R. (2021). Travel risk perception and travel behaviour during the COVID-19 pandemic 2020: a case study of the DACH region. *Current Issues in Tourism*, *24*(7), 1003–1016. https://doi.org/10.1080/13683500.2020.1803807

OCDE. (2020). *Tourism Policy Responses to the coronavirus (COVID-19). June*, 1–50. https://read.oecd-ilibrary.org/view/?ref=124_124984-7uf8nm95se&Title=Covid-19:Tourism Policy Responses

Sánchez-Cañizares, S. M., Cabeza-Ramírez, L. J., Muñoz-Fernández, G., & Fuentes-García, F. J. (2021). Impact of the perceived risk from Covid-19 on intention to travel. *Current Issues in Tourism*, *24*(7), 970–984. https://doi.org/10.1080/13683500.2020.1829571

Tourism Malaysia. (2020). *Survey on Domestic Travel in Malaysia. April.* https://www.tourism.gov.my/files/uploads/DomTravelerSurveyafterMCO4.pdf

UNWTO. (2020). *International Tourism Growth Continues to Outpace the Global Economy.* https://www.unwto.org/international-tourism-and-covid-19

Wang, F., Xue, T., Wang, T., & Wu, B. (2020). The mechanism of tourism risk perception in severe epidemic: The antecedent effect of place image depicted in anti-epidemic music videos and the moderating effect of visiting history. *Sustainability (Switzerland)*, *12*(13). https://doi.org/10.3390/su12135454

Waters, E. A., Ackermann, N., & Wheeler, C. S. (2019). Specifying future behavior when assessing risk perceptions: Implications for measurement and theory. *Medical Decision Making*, *39*(8), 986–997. https://doi.org/10.1177/0272989X19879704

Wen, J., Kozak, M., Yang, S., & Liu, F. (2020). COVID-19: potential effects on Chinese citizens' lifestyle and travel. *Tourism Review*, *May*. https://doi.org/10.1108/TR-03-2020-0110

Williams, C. C. (2020). Impacts of the coronavirus pandemic on Europe's tourism industry: Addressing tourism enterprises and workers in the undeclared economy. *International Journal of Tourism Research*, *June*, 1–10. https://doi.org/10.1002/jtr.2395

Yang, E. C. L., Sharif, S. P., & Khoo-Lattimore, C. (2015). Tourists' risk perception of risky destinations: The case of Sabah's eastern coast. *Tourism and Hospitality Research*, *15*(3), 206–221. https://doi.org/10.1177/1467358415576085

Zhu, H., & Deng, F. (2020). How to influence rural tourism intention by risk knowledge during Covid-19 containment in China: Mediating role of risk perception and attitude. *International Journal of Environmental Research and Public Health*, *17*(10), 3514. https://doi.org/10.3390/ijerph17103514

Appendix 1: Constructs and sources for measurement

Table 7.4 Constructs and sources for the measurement of attitude, subjective norm, perceived behavioural control, behavioural intentions, and risk perception

Variables measuring item		*Source of adoption*
Attitude		
AT1	For me to travel domestically is enjoyable	Chaulagain et al. (2021), Lee et al. (2012)
AT2	For me to travel domestically is beneficial.	
AT3	For me to travel domestically is useful.	
Subjective norm		
SN1	Most people who are important to me travel domestically.	Chaulagain et al. (2021), Lee et al. (2012)
SN2	Most people who are important to me thought that it is a good idea to travel domestically.	
SN3	Most people who are important to me agreed with me to travel domestically.	
Perceived behavioural control		
PBC1	For me to travel domestically is easy.	Lee et al. (2012)
PBC2	I am confident that if I want to, I could travel domestically.	
PBC3	I have enough resources, time and opportunities to travel domestically.	
Behavioural intentions		
BI1	I will plan to travel domestically	Bae and Chang (2021), Lee et al. (2012)
BI2	For me to travel in Malaysia is possible	
BI2	I will invest time and money to travel in Malaysia	
Risk perception		
RP1	How worried are you personally about COVID-19 at present?	Sánchez-Cañizares et al. (2021), Yang et al. (2015)
RP2	I prefer to shorten the duration of my potential trips during the COVID-19 pandemic.	
RP3	It is serious that getting sick with COVID-19.	

Section B

The future of business and economy in the post-COVID-19 era

8 Post-COVID-19 job preparedness in Malaysia

Insights from future jobseekers

Huey Fen Cheong and Cecilia Yin Mei Cheong

8.1 Introduction

After more than a year of battle against the COVID-19 pandemic, 2020 witnessed a total of 1.8 million global deaths (reported by Worldometers, 2021) and 114 million job losses in 'relative to the pre-crisis employment level in 2019' (reported by International Labour Organization/ILO, January 25, 2021). The concerns over mortality and poverty have been evoking global debates between lives and livelihoods in policymaking (reported in *The Star*, Tan, April 18, 2020).

Similarly, in Malaysia, the COVID-19 lockdown had severely affected the job market, and the impact is expected to last for years. According to the Department of Statistics of Malaysia (DOSM; Key Statistics of Labour Force in Malaysia, 2021), Malaysian unemployment has been rising since COVID-19, especially after the first Movement Control Order on March 18, 2020. As shown in Figure 8.1, the number of unemployment rose to an all-time high in May 2020, that is when the first lockdown slowly eased. The year 2020 closed with 772,900 Malaysians unemployed.

As the COVID-19 pandemic continues (as of April 15, 2021), Malaysian unemployment may worsen with the incoming of fresh graduates every year, which will add to the existing unemployment. In 2020, the Higher Education Minister Datuk Seri Noraini Ahmad announced that 75,000 or 25% fresh graduates of 2020 were expected to be unemployed (reported in *Malay Mail*, Dzulkifly, September 28, 2020). Nevertheless, the 2020 cohorts were delayed due to COVID-19. Hence, when the second Movement Control Order/MCO 2.0 was enforced the next year from January 13 to March 4, 2021, Malaysian Employers Federation executive director Datuk Shamsuddin Bardan suggested policymakers consider around 1 million fresh graduates in 2021 – from both 2020 and 2021 cohorts – who will be entering the job market (reported in *The Star*, Tan, January 13, 2021).

DOI: 10.4324/9781003182740-8

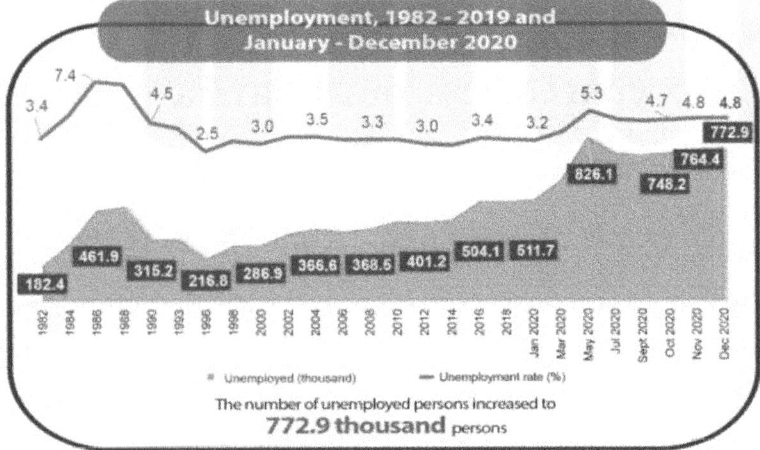

Figure 8.1 Unemployment in Malaysia before (1982-2019) and during (2020) COVID-19

Source: Department of Statistics of Malaysia's December 2020 report.

The latest news was the drastic decrease of fresh graduates' salaries, which according to DOSM, the majority earning decreased from RM2,001-RM2,500 in 2019 to RM1,001-RM1,500 in 2020 (reported in Free Malaysia Today, April 2, 2021). As stated in *Malay Mail*'s headline, 'For at least a decade, monthly wage as low as RM1,000 the norm for Malaysian fresh grads' (reported on April 14, 2021), also published the statistics (see Figure 8.2).

This chapter aims to understand Malaysian university students during the COVID-19 pandemic, particularly on their perspectives and preparedness towards entering the next phase, the job market, after they graduated from the university. The study employed Gibbs' reflective cycle (1988), which was also used in other COVID-19-related studies to uncover different individuals' perspectives and experiences during this challenging time (Ayedee & Kumar, 2020; Hill & Fitzgerald, 2020; Rodham et al., 2020). Unlike the common viewpoint-based studies (e.g., surveys, focus groups, and interviews), Gibb provides step-by-step self-reflection (see Section 8.2) to the participants, who not only reflect on their experiences but also analyse them and propose ways to overcome and/or improve similar experiences in the future.

We studied 58 *well-informed participants* who researched the *new-and-still-changing* job market around March–November 2020 before performing *well-thought, in-depth reflections* based on the newly found, updated knowledge. This overcomes the weaknesses of past studies, which studied participants' general views using the quantitative approach/questionnaire surveys (Ahmad, 2020; Kamaruddin, Ahmad, Husain, & Abd Hamid,

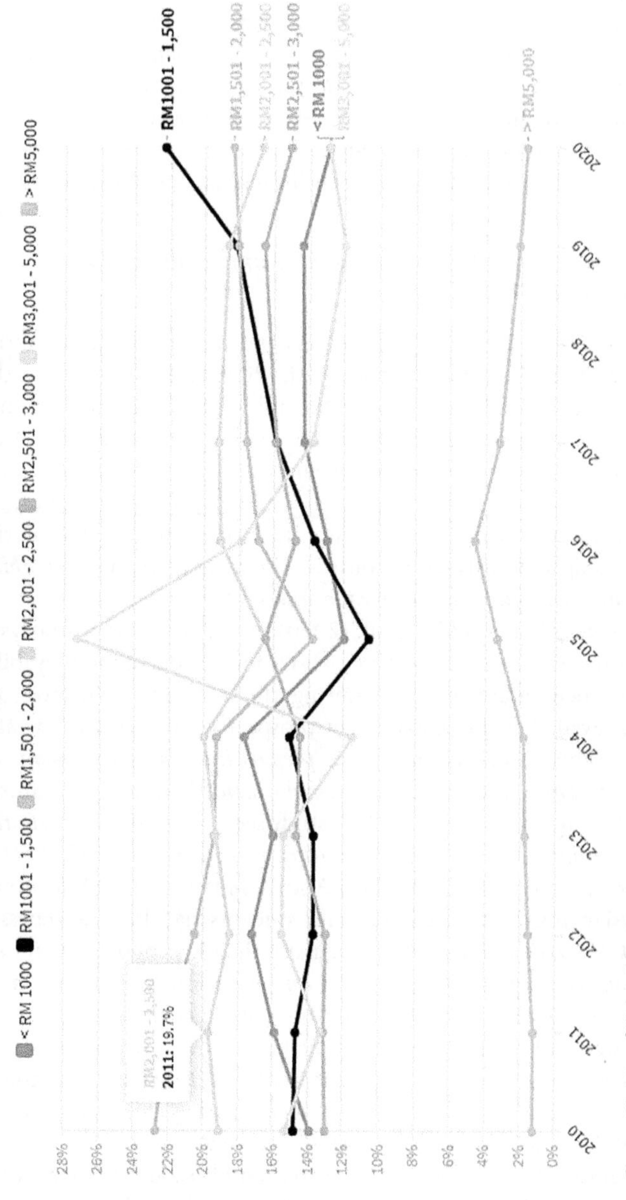

Figure 8.2 Income range for Malaysian fresh graduates (2010–2020)
Source: *Malay Mail* (Lim and Ayamany, April 14, 2021).

2020) and small scale, 10-informant interviews (Abd Rahman, Ismail, Ridzuan, & Abd Samad, 2020).

Our study on the *future* jobseekers further contributes to the existing literature that only focuses on the *current* jobseekers in Malaysia, who were fresh graduates or close-graduates (final-year students) (Abd Rahman et al., 2020; Kamaruddin et al., 2020) or students of any stages on gig jobs (Ahmad, 2020). While the past studies asked for perspectives on the *current* COVID-19 job market, our study extends the inquiries to the future outlook of the job market, which, hopefully, will be post-COVID-19.

8.1.1 The future outlook: Graduates' job hunting during and beyond COVID-19

The rising unemployment raises questions and doubts about the future of university graduates. Abd Rahman et al. (2020) interviews found that Malaysian graduates had not changed their mindsets for the new job market, which would worsen unemployment. Most graduates preferred the common job hunting, while only a few chose entrepreneurship, but none mentioned gig work. Abd Rahman et al. emphasised the importance of tertiary education in changing university students' mindsets and offering entrepreneurship and skills-based courses. *This seems to imply employability courses to teach new mindsets, knowledge, and skills.*

Another study, Kamaruddin et al. (2020) survey, shows that Malaysian final-year university students were ready for graduate employability courses and their internship even during the lockdown. However, the students believed that the employment prospect would remain low after COVID-19. This seems to imply that *preparedness for employment and employability courses may not lead to employment.* Unlike Abd Rahman et al. (2020), Kamaruddin et al. (2020) study seem to *question the effectiveness of employability courses in solving unemployment even after COVID-19.*

However, Ahmad (2020) [and also Abd Rahman et al. (2020)] found that Malaysian university graduates and students had low awareness of the new COVID-19 job market, particularly the gig economy. *This raises doubts on the participants' reflections in any viewpoint-based studies about the COVID-19 job market.* Ahmad (2020) stressed the importance of having knowledge and skills to overcome the new normal, which may last in the 'post-pandemic period' (p. 45), that is after COVID-19. She stressed upskilling and reskilling, which have been gaining popularity during COVID-19. *This calls back for employability courses.*

As such, unlike the common viewpoint-based studies, our participants were well-informed with a higher awareness of the new job market, as they surveyed about it themselves. They could better reflect the new mindsets, knowledge and skills, which are in demand in the new job market. This further helps them in reflecting their preparedness in entering the job market as well as the effectiveness of employability courses. The latter includes the job preparation course in which this study was derived (see the next section).

8.2 Method

This study derives from a COVID-19-related assignment, which was designed for a job preparation course at a Malaysian university to prepare the students/participants for the COVID-19 job market. The course teaches job application skills, such as researching the self and job market, searching for jobs, writing resumes and cover letters, performing interviews, etc.

The job market surveys and reflections were conducted around October–November 2020, which covers the COVID-19 job market since the first lockdown in March 2020. In other words, the surveys and reflections cover the job market around March–November 2020. After almost a year, we witnessed more COVID-19 effects as well as more knowledge about it from the increasing research and experts' reviews. This made it a good timing to survey about the COVID-19 job market and reflect on it. The students' surveys were presented in class, and their reflections were written in *reflective essays.* Such an open-ended approach welcomed all possibilities of information/knowledge, thoughts, and feelings.

8.2.1 Research design

This qualitative, reflective analysis uses Gibbs' reflective cycle (1988), which consists of 6 steps: description, feelings, evaluation, analysis, conclusion, and action plan. The first 3 steps (description, feelings, and evaluation) focus on what happened. The last 3 steps (analysis, conclusion, and action plan) lead the individuals to reflect on the ways to improve and/or solve. *Most viewpoint-based studies only cover the first 3 steps.*

The procedure of the study can be summarised into these six steps.

8.2.1.1 Description

The participants (in groups of 3–5) surveyed related information about the COVID-19 job market in 5 resources or aspects:

- a News article (Group 1)
- b Academic publication or other media sources (Group 2)
- c Job portals, advertisements, resources, and websites (Group 3)
- d Industry Experts' advice on job-hunting and increasing self-employability (Group 4)
- e Malaysian government's and institutions' policies and strategies (Group 5)

The participants presented their findings to all participants within the same class through live or pre-recorded *presentations* and began their *reflective essays* with:

> What have you learnt or not learnt from yours and others' surveys?

This question investigates useful and/or necessary knowledge for jobseekers. The presentations were not merely presenting the information available or the participants' survey findings. It was intentionally filtered and reorganised for their meaningful knowledge and presentation. From surveys and presentations to reflections on what they had (not) learnt, there were three screenings of importance among future jobseekers. This step ensures that all participants were well-informed for the following reflections.

8.2.1.2 Feelings

The participants expressed their feelings as future jobseekers by answering:

> Are you prepared for the post-COVID-19 job market (based on what you have learnt)?

8.2.1.3 Evaluation

The participants evaluated and justified their answers in *Step 2: Feelings:*

> Why are you prepared or not prepared for the post-COVID-19 job market?

8.2.1.4 Analysis

The participants thought of ways to overcome their unpreparedness.

8.2.1.5 Conclusion

The participants related their reflections to the job preparation course, which turned their assignments into this research. They answered the question: 'What do you hope to learn from this course in preparing you for the post-COVID-19 job market? Why?'

8.2.1.6 Action plan

The participants thought of ways to overcome the post-COVID-19 job market in the future as jobseekers.

8.2.2 The participants

The participants were third-year undergraduate students who attended a job preparation course at a Malaysian university in Semester 1 (Session 2020/2021), that is from October 2020 to January 2021. They were future jobseekers, who would be entering internship a year later, around October 2021 and officially entering the job market after their graduation in 2022, which, hopefully, will be post-COVID-19. This combination made them a good candidate to reflect on both the current COVID-19 job market and also the future post-COVID-19 job market, which will be affected by post-COVID-19 effects.

There were a total of 64 students from 3 classes of the job preparation course. However, two types of students were excluded from the research: (1) non-Malaysian students and (2) students who did not give their consent to participate in the study. After the exclusion, this study had a total of 58 participants from Class 1 (12), Class 2 (26), and Class 3 (20). The students were all from the same discipline, that is studying languages and linguistics.

The research used both *convenience* and *purposive* sampling. It was convenience sampling, as the participants and data were all taken from a job preparation course, specifically from its assignment. Nevertheless, the participants' reflections were based on their own as well as their classmates' survey findings, which might differ among 3 classes. As such, we analysed both survey findings and reflections in 3 groups, according to the classes.

As for why it is purposive sampling, we studied participants from the job preparation course, which was catered specifically for a particular faculty/ discipline, that is linguistics.

8.2.3 Scope and limitation

Like any qualitative study, this study worked on a small scale for in-depth analysis and understanding. It only focused on students majoring in languages and linguistics, which was not representative of other disciplines. While linguistics was a convenient choice, it was also a good choice for being versatile or employable in various industries. Also, the study only focused on one university, which again was not representative of all universities.

Nevertheless, this study may serve as a preliminary study for future research on a larger scale.

8.3 Findings

As surveys and presentations were conducted in each class independently, the survey findings and reflections of students/participants showed both similarities and differences across three classes. This provides meaningful insights into the relationship between future jobseekers' knowledge and job preparedness.

Below are the findings presented according to the steps in Gibb's (1988) reflective cycle (see Section 8.2.1).

8.3.1 *Description: What have you learnt or not learnt from yours and others' surveys?*

The participants' surveys and presentations uncovered changes in the job market, that is the new normal. Besides the changing working environment and increasing unemployment, they also presented new job opportunities and training. The reflection on what they have (not) learnt investigates information/knowledge about the post-COVID-19 job market, which was found useful and/or necessary by future jobseekers. This chapter presents 4 key findings.

8.3.1.1 What is/are new?

From Class 1, most participants were fascinated by the new terms and concepts (to them). Some responses on the gig market and autonomous enterprises include *'learnt new important terms'* and *'was totally unaware of earlier'*. Nevertheless, they were aware of their potential to be the new normal: *'These terms might soon be the reality and norm of the post-COVID-19 job market.'* They were also fascinated by the new abnormal, which was normal pre-COVID, for example working on-site/WoS: *'There are still companies that don't allow their employees to do remote working. I found it unusual because most people I'm surrounded with are all working at home.'*

Although Class 1 had low awareness of the COVID-19 job market theoretically (from readings), they were sensitive, practically, to the new ab/normal from their surroundings and also able to see the post-COVID-19 possibilities. Nevertheless, the former ensured a more accurate, detailed, and in-depth knowledge from readings. Although they were not too welcoming towards the new normal, they were aware that knowledge about it was necessary to prepare themselves for the future job market:

> I learnt about a new term called gig market and how it is the new normal of future employment. It's new and not very appealing as well for me to think that I have to adapt to a new situation where I can't expect to have a permanent job, but at least, having heard this news, I can prepare myself for the future.

Class 2 took an interest in the new practices (to them) in the working environment, for example the hybrid approach – 'alternating employees that go to the office, while the other half work at home', and in the job application, for example virtual interviews and the pain letter approach. Also, there was a minority of participants who perceived gig jobs as part-time jobs:

> gig work is important amid and post COVID-19 era, simply because one's main job does not guarantee to pay all of one's bills. One must take gig work to make ends meet, or else it would be hard to survive, more so if one lives in the big city.

Even gig jobs will be redefined from part-time jobs to the *new normal* jobs, that is the main jobs. Nevertheless, few participants wanted to learn about other alternatives, rather than totally believing in the industry experts and media:

> alternative ways to find jobs
>
> other options other than entrepreneurship and gigs as a solution because not everyone has the skills and patience to even do one
>
> What type of job vacancies do not need future employees to have knowledge in digital skills? I might not land a job that needs digital skills, as it is very competitive.

Class 3, however, focused on the new demands in the new job market (see Section 8.3.1.3).

To sum up, all participants were only made aware of the new normal (including new demands) after they surveyed for information. Nevertheless, some were alert, sensitive, and observant, which helped them to sense the changes, though vaguely, from their surroundings. Also, some could think critically and out of the box. All these would likely influence their job preparedness. Second, the new normal was not something new, but something less common in the past (pre-COVID) that was becoming more common and thus, the new normal.

8.3.1.2 What has/have existed? (What remain(s) important?)

Both Class 1 and Class 2 participants generally showed low awareness of online job portals, which have existed pre-COVID. Besides the popular JobStreet, they learnt the existence of other portals such as Maukerja, WOBB, Indeed, FastJobs, Seek Asia, and Intern.My. Almost all participants in Class 1 hoped to learn how to use those portals, as they may affect their job hunting. Class 2, however, was more interested to learn how to build an online presence, for example through LinkedIn.

Besides new knowledge and skills, some old job-hunting skills remain important to jobseekers to prepare for the post-COVID-19 job market. When COVID-19-related studies are preoccupied with COVID-19-related changes, they tend to neglect the pre-COVID-19 elements that remain relevant. Again, the findings question the past studies about job preparedness during COVID-19. Could their preparedness be affected by non- or pre-COVID-19 (existing) issues?

After this research in 2020, a few job portals such as JobStreet and WOBB made COVID-19-related transformations around January 2021, for example using AI, machine learning, and virtual interviews. See the updates on the Facebook group, *the post-COVID-19 job market in Malaysia*, https://www.facebook.com/hashtag/newjobportal/?__gid__=2805574166392321. The skills of using job portals remain important and need to be incorporated and updated in employability courses, which are increasing to solve unemployment during COVID-19.

Nevertheless, the different learning interests between Class 1 and Class 2, that is between using job portals and building an online presence, demonstrated different mentalities among future jobseekers. Class 1 focused on finding and applying for jobs, whereas Class 2 focused on attracting jobs, as they claimed, 'marketing ourselves'. Online presence has gained importance in job-hunting skills, especially with LinkedIn. This may be accelerated due to COVID-19.

Again, Class 3's reflections were mainly on the market demands (see the next section).

8.3.1.3 What is/are in demand?

The third interest is the demands in the new job market. Class 1 was eager to learn 'jobs', 'job types', and 'types of works' in demand, which they used interchangeably. They learnt three in-demand job types: gigs, digital, and self-driven (e.g., using AI and machine learning). However, many hoped to learn more about the *specific* fields and jobs in demand, so they can relate them to their study majors. Some blamed the overemphasis of digital jobs for overshadowing information about other job types. Second, they wanted to learn about the 'how': how to get in-demand jobs, that is the criteria. This includes learning digital skills to increase their employability in the job market, which is moving towards digitalisation. To sum up, Class 1 seemed to demonstrate a demand for more *concrete knowledge*, which specifies the particular fields and jobs in demand, which they could apply, as well as specifies the ways to get jobs.

Class 2 showed a different perspective, as the participants thought about job losses and job opportunities (also, jobs in demand), while optimistically focusing more on the latter. Like Class 1, they were aware of the demand for digital jobs and skills. Nevertheless, they learnt from the info presenters to be willing to accept any jobs, even those not within their majors. They stressed the willingness to accept, to adapt, and to change the mindset, for example:

> I have also learnt that we should not be picky and choosy when applying for jobs, especially during this pandemic where the number of unemployment is currently increasing. If we still firmly believe that some jobs are not suitable for us, we should change that mindset.
>
> We must also show willingness to adapt, which means taking unskilled jobs outside of our educational expertise.

Following the previous two classes, Class 3 further emphasised the demand for digital jobs and skills, including those related to their linguistic majors, for example online translation services and online language teaching. Despite the challenges to finding jobs, some expressed perseverance to 'not give up'.

Among all demands, the main one was on digital skills and digital-related jobs. Nevertheless, this section also reveals the mindsets in demand, that is adaptability, willingness to change, and perseverance. Class 2 showed that jobseekers' mindsets could be affected by the way job market info was presented to them, besides willing to change their mindsets themselves. This may be the answer to past research findings, which lamented that graduates had not changed their mindsets for the COVID-19 job market (i.e., Abd Rahman et al., 2020).

8.3.1.4 What had been done?

The participants also learned the government initiatives in overcoming the challenging job market. These include providing financial aids and upskilling courses.

All classes showed low awareness of the various initiatives: 'I was quite surprised', 'I had no idea', and 'I was not aware of', as well as 'I realise' and 'I found out' (from the survey). Some heard of only a few prominent ones (especially PenjanaKerjaya and Kita Prihatin) and without understanding the details. One participant from Class 3 called for more publicity on such initiatives, as 'the information is little known by the people'. Second, some also showed appreciation, especially to the government:

> These efforts can at least reduce the burden of Malaysians and help them to recover back their losses. Despite Malaysia facing a weak

> economy and financial issues, the government is still helping the citizens. From this, I learnt that we, as Malaysians, need to be grateful, never give up and stay positive while going through this challenging life without complaining.

However, some hoped to learn about the effectiveness of those initiatives. Some asked for feedback:

> It would be fascinating to know some feedback from those that have used these incentives and whether the incentives are effective for university students.

Some questioned the effective use of the budget behind those initiatives:

> I would like to know about the whole budget that was set by the government to help the unemployed and how they are going to utilize it as well as possible and would this following budget really help in decreasing the unemployment rate.

Some saw these as short-term relief but not a solution (i.e., employment):

> As great as the initiatives are, it did not give me a sense of security as there is no guarantee that even with these initiatives, I will be able to get a job.

Overall, all classes showed similar responses to government initiatives: low awareness, high appreciation, but in doubt. They might have low awareness of COVID-19 news, including reports about government initiatives, but they were aware of the COVID-19 reality and would not take the media reports for granted.

In conclusion, this section confirms the past studies on the low awareness/knowledge of university graduates and students about the new COVID-19 job market. Instead of getting views from them about the subject that they were not familiar with or merely knew generally as 'new normal', this section led the participants to gather information themselves from various media and present explicit, concrete knowledge about the new normal. This new normal was presented in 4 sub-sections: Section 8.3.1.1 on new terms, concepts, and practices (What is/are new?); Section 8.3.1.2 on ongoing practices from pre-COVID-19 (What has/have existed?); Section 8.3.1.3 on the new and ongoing demands (What is/are in demand?); and Section 8.3.1.4 on new initiatives (What had been done?). The findings show that the term 'new normal' does not necessarily mean something new that did not exist before COVID-19 but means things – new or old – that become *normal* in the new COVID-19 era.

8.3.2 *Feelings: Are you prepared for the post-COVID-19 job market (based on what you have learnt)?*

Participants from all classes showed mixed responses to job preparedness. In Class 1 of 12 students/participants, only 2 were prepared for the post-COVID-19 job market, while the rest claimed unprepared. In Class 2 of 26 participants, however, the situation seemed to be better: 7 were prepared, 11 were unprepared, while 8 were in between. Almost similar to Class 2, in Class 3 of 20 participants, 7 were prepared, 11 were unprepared, while 2 were in between.

Most past studies focused on the participants' feelings towards the new normal (see Section 8.1.1) but rarely reflected on their own feelings (see the next section).

8.3.3 *Evaluation: Why are you prepared or not prepared for the post-COVID-19 job market?*

All classes showed a strong relationship between knowledge and job preparedness. This reinforces our earlier arguments about the importance of knowledge about the new job market towards one's job preparedness. Nevertheless, mindset mediates between knowledge and preparedness.

8.3.3.1 *Knowledge and preparedness*

1 Knowledge gives courage and hope:

> I have gained a lot from this survey research. I could not deny that I was a little sceptical and scared to enter the new working phase, especially in the post-COVID-19 future. But by doing this survey, it lifted my spirit and brings hope in me that there are job opportunities out there waiting for me even during these tough times. Even if there are no job opportunities in my field, I should not lose hope and I should try new things and discover my new self.
>
> (Class 1; similar responses from Class 2)

2 Knowledge gives guide and direction:

> Yes, I am prepared for the post-COVID-19 job market. This is because I have gained lots of information and knowledge from all the presentations done by my fellow classmates which will be helpful for job hunting in future… All these inputs serve as guidance for me to

shift my focus towards elevating my employability by being aware of the changes that occur in the job industry and how to overcome it.

(Class 1; similar responses from Classes 2 and 3)

3 Mindset mediates between knowledge and preparedness.
Besides knowledge, mindset influences one's preparedness. Points 1 and 2 embed optimism, that is to believe in opportunities in challenging times and changing perspective from problems to solutions. A more explicit example:

I would be more prepared for entering the job market by focusing on the jobs and opportunities that are still available, rather than lamenting on the unfortunate situation caused by the pandemic.

(Class 2)

Another good mindset that contributes to job preparedness is adaptability:

I would say that I have prepared because one needs to be more flexible in terms of self-ability.

(Class 2)

If there's no suitable job for me related to my studies, GrabFood or Foodpanda is a good way to start. The demand for food delivery has been skyrocketing since the pandemic. The other job.is IT...Since making our own product(s) can support myself, this time during this pandemic, I could [venture into entrepreneurship].

(Class 3)

8.3.3.2 Knowledge and unpreparedness

Nevertheless, knowledge may also cause unpreparedness.

1 Knowledge about the market demand vs. knowledge about the self: They felt themselves not up to the expectation of the market (Class 1; Points a and c) and the self (Class 2; Points b and d):

a 'I don't have': The common responses in Class 1 were 'lack':

I don't think I am prepared or properly equipped for the post-COVID-19 job market. One major and common information that I learned from all the presentations is that most job opportunities will be in the information technology, software, online marketing, and e-commerce fields. All these fields require great digital skills, which I feel I lack.

b 'I need more': More responses from Class 2 were about 'enhanced', 'sharpen', and 'mastered' certain skills:

> They pointed out gig economy and entrepreneurship in their presentation. I believe these types of jobs require high independence and adaptability skills which I still need to sharpen.

c High expectation of the job market: Some guessed or overestimated the market demand.

Many in Class 1 thought that the job market needs certain skills at high levels: 'like an expert', 'the standard of professionals', 'the advanced level', and 'high confidence and patience'.

d High expectation of the self, though also in relation to the market demand.

Many responses in Class 2 were about not 'completely', 'fully', 'enough', and 'thoroughly' 'equip' themselves with the necessary skills.

2 Knowledge about the demotivating situation.

Some students in Class 2 lamented about unemployment, high competitiveness, and affected industries.

3 Again, mindset mediates between knowledge and preparedness.

Point 1 largely depends on one's self-confidence, while Point 2 relates to one's optimism.

To sum up, the above findings seem to challenge the cliché, 'knowledge is power'. Ironically, knowledge can empower and also disempower.

8.3.3.3 No knowledge and unpreparedness

However, without knowledge, the unknown caused uncertainties and thus, unpreparedness.

1 The unknown future of gigs and entrepreneurship: The common responses were 'risky':

> As for the gig market, one should be mentally prepared to enter such a risky market.
>
> (Class 1)

> Honestly, I'm not truly prepared for the post-COVID-19 job market, especially after knowing that the government encourages the new

> generation to be more active in businesses. We all know the risk we have to face when we decide to be a trader.
>
> (Class 1)

2 The unknown future of the job market:

> After hearing from all the groups and their surveys, I am still not prepared to face the job market. My reasoning for stating so is that we do not know what the future has in store for us. The materials presented in this session may not be relevant within a few months. Until months before I have to face the job market, only then I must prepare myself for it.
>
> (Class 1; similar responses from Classes 2 and 3.)

3 The unknown self, for example uncertain about the job/career they wanted (Class 3).

8.3.3.4 No knowledge and preparedness

Nevertheless, one participant from Class 3 showed that the unknown future might also lead to job preparedness, with the help of a positive mindset:

> I am ready for the post-COVID-19 job market. This is because, by that time, I believe that job demands from every sector has finally increased.

8.3.4 Analysis: How to increase job preparedness?

To increase their job preparedness, all participants emphasised upskilling themselves, particularly in digital skills that are in demand. They could not ensure employment, but they could ensure employability.

This is another part which is rarely addressed in previous studies (see Section 8.1.1), that is involving the participants in problem-solving. Problem-solving is usually thought and/or done by the powerful (e.g., the government) and the knowledgeable (knowledge experts). This section and the coming two sections showed that the jobseekers could be involved in problem-solving too.

8.3.5 Conclusion: What do you hope to learn from this course in preparing you for the post-COVID-19 job market? Why?

As for the job preparation course, which turned their assignments into this research, all classes suggested similar things:

a *Technical skills of job application*
Although the above were included in this course, the participants asked for updated skills to suit the current digitalised context, that is from the conventional paper resume to video resume, from physical interviews to virtual interviews, etc. The digital forms contain different sets of skills and etiquettes. Class 2 emphasised building an online presence and networking through LinkedIn, which could also serve as a digital resume and job portal.

b *Soft skills*
The participants emphasised teamwork and interpersonal skills, but, surprisingly, not leadership skills.

c *Skills for the post-COVID-19 job market*
Any skills that address the new normal in the job application and at the workplace.

d *Knowledge/Skills related to their majors*
Due to the rising unemployment, they hoped to learn about the updates of job opportunities related to their majors. (Except Class 3, which presentations related to the linguistic major.)

e *Employability courses are gaining popularity during COVID-19 but rarely researched.* This section on one employability course may serve as a preliminary to future research on other employability courses.

8.3.6 Action plan: How to overcome the challenges in the post-COVID-19 job market?

Many participants did not have action plans other than upskilling and reskilling themselves (see Section 8.3.4). It was mainly due to the uncertain post-COVID-19 job market, where the participants had about a year before entering:

> I believe things are still very uncertain and this uncertainty definitely affects my plans to land my potential jobs in the future. With so many changes happening constantly, I believe predicting my future job market is something extremely tricky. Who's to say how the situation will be in the future? Will it be worse? Better? Another question that comes to my mind when I think of the term "post-COVID-19" is, how will our nation look like after COVID-19? Will the current norm still be practised to prevent the pandemic from surging? In that case, what will the working life look like? Which jobs will be in the market then? With so many questions being left unanswered, I believe I cannot firmly say that I am ready for the job market in the future or even plan for it.
>
> (Class 2)

Nevertheless, some participants from Class 3 proposed the steps to get a job. However, the focus remained on upskilling and reskilling, while the rest was the basic job application process:

1 *Understanding the job scope*
2 *Adding and improving skill*
3 *Start job searching online*
4 *Preparing a specific resume and cover letter*
5 *Prepare for job interviews*

8.4 Conclusion

This study shows that local university students had low awareness of the COVID-19 job market until they conducted the surveys. However, some could sense the changes, though vaguely, from their surroundings. Also, some could think critically for alternatives that might overcome the challenging job market, not following the common advice on gigs and entrepreneurship. They even questioned the effectiveness of government initiatives in solving unemployment. Besides displaying different mindsets, the mindsets of these future jobseekers could change according to the way the COVID-19 job market was presented to them.

As for job preparedness, the study shows mixed responses. It discovers the strong relationship between knowledge and job preparedness, while mindset (e.g., optimism/pessimism, willingness to change, and perseverance) mediates between them. Job preparedness also mediates between knowledge about the job market and knowledge about the self, as illustrated in Figure 8.3. One will be more prepared if he/she knows that the self can fulfil the demands in, and overcome the challenges of, the job market. Nevertheless, knowledge can empower and also disempower jobseekers.

As such, this study questions the past studies on jobseekers, in which the participants/jobseekers were even found having low awareness of the COVID-19 job market. Also, it challenges the simple, unidirectional perspective on jobseekers' awareness of the COVID-19 job market, their job preparedness, and their mindsets. See Section 8.1.2 for the related literature.

After the COVID-19 job market survey and reflections, the students knew that they could not ensure employment, but they could strive to ensure employability. They emphasised upskilling and reskilling while having problems planning for the unpredictable job market.

For future research, we recommend action research, which could provide solid solutions or strategies to overcome the challenging job market. Or, at least, it could test the effectiveness of the proposed solutions or

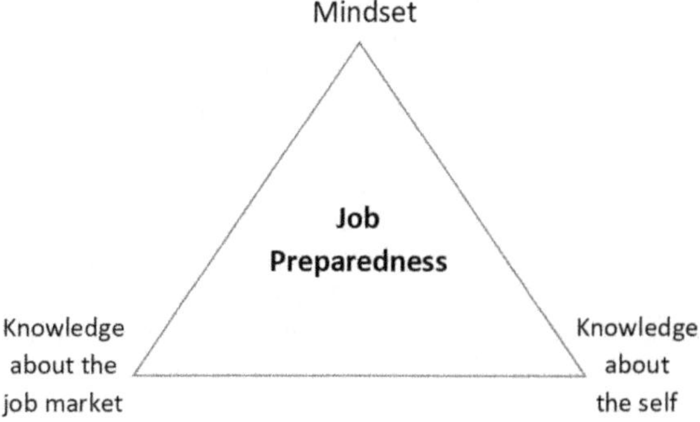

Figure 8.3 The relationship of job preparedness, knowledge, and mindset

strategies (see Section 8.3.1.4 on the participants' curiosity towards the effectiveness of the government's initiatives). Also, this small-scale study (on linguistic students) can be expanded to a larger scale that involves students or future jobseekers from more disciplines.

Summary

- Participants of COVID-19-related research require sufficient COVID-19 related knowledge to contribute, especially for viewpoint-based research.
- Job preparedness: Mediates between knowledge about the job market and knowledge about the self.
- Relationship between knowledge and job preparedness: Mediated by mindsets.
- Mindsets for job preparedness: Optimism, willingness to change, and perseverance.
- Focus on *employability:* Willingness to upskill and reskill as plans in preparation for unpredictable *employment.*

References

Abd Rahman, N. H., Ismail, S., Ridzuan, A. R., & Abd Samad, K. (2020). Graduates' mindset in designing their initial career. *International Journal of Academic Research in Business and Social Sciences, 10.* doi:10.6007/IJARBSS/v10-i10/7798

Ahmad, N. (2020). Gig economy: The future of working. *International Journal of Communication, Management and Humanities, 1*(2), 45–52.

Ayedee, N., & Kumar, A. (2020). Indian education system and growing number of online conferences: scenario under COVID-19. *Asian Journal of Management, 11*(4), 395–401.

Coronavirus Death Toll. (2021, February 7). Retrieved from https://www.worldometers.info/coronavirus/coronavirus-death-toll/

COVID-19 and the world of work: updated estimates and analysis. (2021, January 25). *ILO Monitor – 7th Edition*, pp. 1–35. Retrieved from International Labour Organization/ILO: https://www.ilo.org/wcmsp5/groups/public/—dgreports/—dcomm/documents/briefingnote/wcms_767028.pdf

Dzulkifly, D. (2020, September 28). Higher education minister foresees 75,000 fresh grads struggling to get jobs in Covid-19 era. *Malay Mail.* Retrieved from https://www.malaymail.com/news/malaysia/2020/09/28/higher-education-minister-foresees-75000-fresh-grads-struggling-to-get-jobs/1907493

Gibbs, G. (1988). Learning by doing: a guide to teaching and learning methods. *Further Education Unit.*

Hill, K., & Fitzgerald, R. (2020). Student perspectives of the impact of COVID-19 on learning. *All Ireland Journal of Higher Education*, *12*(2): 1–9.

Kamaruddin, M. I. H., Ahmad, A., Husain, M. A., & Abd Hamid, S. N. (2020). Graduate employability post-COVID-19: The case of a Malaysian public university. *Higher Education, Skills and Work-Based Learning*, *11*(3): 710-724.

Key Statistics of Labour Force in Malaysia, December 2020. (2021, February 8). Retrieved from Department of Statistics of Malaysia (DOSM): https://www.dosm.gov.my/v1/index.php?r=column/cthemeByCat&cat=124&bul_id=RDllTkpHejRFNGlRdlRLWWJzMi91QT09&menu_id=Tm8zcnRjdVRNWWlpWjRlbmtlaDk1UT09

Lim, I., & Ayamany, K. (2021, April 14). For at least a decade, monthly wage as low as RM1,000 the norm for Malaysian fresh grads. *Malay Mail.* Retrieved from https://www.malaymail.com/news/malaysia/2021/04/14/for-at-least-a-decade-monthly-wage-as-low-as-rm1000-the-norm-for-malaysian/1966262

Low salaries for grads only temporary, say employers. (2021, April 2). *Free Malaysia Today.* Retrieved from https://www.freemalaysiatoday.com/category/nation/2021/04/02/low-salaries-for-grads-only-temporary-say-employers/?fbclid=IwAR3IQvdqC59InYgF1-nicKH05GZd-EhHCk-8k-o9NrVvE3jG0m2zZ3cbFXA

Rodham, K., Bains, K., Westbrook, J., Stanulewicz, N., Byrne-Davis, L., Hart, J., & Chater, A. (2020). Rapid review: reflective practice in crisis situations.

Tan, R. (2021, January 13). Risk of rising unemployment remains high with MCO 2.0. *The Star.* Retrieved from https://www.thestar.com.my/business/business-news/2021/01/13/risk-of-rising-unemployment-remains-high-with-mco-20

Tan, T. H. (2020, April 18). Lives versus livelihoods in the face of pandemic. *The Star.* Retrieved from https://www.thestar.com.my/business/business-news/2020/04/18/lives-versus-livelihoods-in-the-face-of-pandemic

9 Re-thinking post-COVID-19 career success

Insights from contemporary career approaches

Chorng Yuan Fung and Asanka Gunasekara

9.1 Introduction

Since the first industrial revolution, the world of work evolves at an exponential rate. As we write this book chapter, employers and employees around the globe are actively trying to find new ways of living and working because of the new challenges the COVID-19 pandemic presents to the world. Individuals are now starting to understand the traditional approach to a career in which organisations were responsible for the career advancement of employees is less relevant, neither the concept of life-long careers within one organisation is (Randstad, n.d.). From the beginning of the pandemic up to November 2020, approximately 764,400 employees in the Malaysian workforce have lost their jobs (Department of Statistics Malaysia, 2021), and more than 100,000 companies of all sizes had to close their businesses (Kuriakose & Tran, 2020), with the spillover effect on the physical, financial and mental health of victims and their families. This could be considered as a wake-up call for the Malaysian workforce as to how they can better be prepared for future employment challenges they face.

The objective of this chapter is to discuss challenges that employees in Malaysia face during the pandemic and to provide a theoretical framework for researchers, HR practitioners and career counsellors in Malaysia to explore how contemporary career approaches can be potential solutions for issues relating to career management and employability in VUCA (volatile, uncertain, complex and ambiguous) environment. In doing this, we have drawn from generally westernised two metaphorical career concepts – protean and boundaryless career theories, alongside of Hirschi's (2012) career resources model, career adaptability and career well-being constructs (Bravo et al., 2017; Briscoe & Hall, 2006; Sullivan & Arthur, 2006; Wiernik & Kostal, 2019). We thought it is more appropriate to conduct this study in a country like Malaysia because (1) there is a

DOI: 10.4324/9781003182740-9

dearth in this area of research that focuses on employees in Asian countries (e.g., Nishanthi & Kailasapathay, 2017) and (2) employees in Asian countries still depend on traditional organisational career orientation (Kiong & Yin-Fah, 2016; Nathan, 2020; Supeli & Creed, 2016). To cover this gap in research, desktop research was carried out to search for conceptual papers, empirical studies as well as news reports in the area of career in the Malaysian context to provide a comprehensive review of this topic.

9.2 Literature review

9.2.1 Definitions for study constructs

Career orientations are the approaches that individuals take in managing and advancing their careers. It is described as the features of work that define one's career goals, reflecting the individual's self-concept regarding his or her self-perceived values, interests, experience, skills and abilities (Bravo et al., 2017, p. 503). Boundaryless career orientation refers to "a state of physical and psychological readiness to move across organisational boundaries when the opportunities arise" (Briscoe & Hall, 2006, p. 5). Boundaryless approach emphasises two types of mobility: (1) physical mobility – which refers to transition across boundaries or actual movements across jobs, firms, occupations and countries and (2) psychological mobility – the perception or the mindset of the career actor of the capacity to make transitions. Individuals with a boundaryless career mindset thus are adaptable, ready to change, learn new things and explore opportunities beyond their traditional work settings. Therefore, acquiring marketable new skills, competencies, knowledge and developing new networks of contacts are prerequisites of the boundaryless career orientation (Lo Presti et al., 2018).

On the other hand, protean career orientation proposes that individuals prefer to take responsibility for their own career outcomes and development, to make decisions based on their intrinsic values to pursue subjective career success and well-being (Briscoe & Hall., 2006). Like boundaryless, protean career approach has two main elements to it: (1) the self-directed nature - individuals who adopt a protean orientation are flexible and adaptable towards their performance and learning demands and (2) the value-driven nature – they use their own personal values to guide and measure their individual perspectives on career success (Briscoe & Hall, 2006, p. 5). Thus, the protean orientation is rather considered as a mindset or an attitude towards one's own career, looking at work in the context of a person's life as a whole, that reflects self-direction and freedom to make choices based on an individual's intrinsic values. Moreover, Hirschi, Jaensch & Herrmann (2017) underline that the protean approach focuses on one's personal values and sense of purpose or calling in life achieved through one's career, rather than on objective success factors such as pay, promotion and power that are predominantly determined by external parties. Individuals who follow protean career orientation are capable of defining career priorities and their career identity while continuing to learn and adapt to any performance demands in a challenging work environment. The relevance of contemporary career orientation in the current Malaysian environment is further discussed next.

9.2.2 The relevance of contemporary career approaches

From the beginning of 2020, COVID-19 poses a series of challenges and complex questions to the world; Malaysia is not an exemption. It has already caused significant changes to the way people in Malaysia think about their future careers. Many people lost their jobs, some will have to redesign the way they pursue the future of work, and some may maintain multi-directional careers to retain in the workforce (Surendran, 2020). Evidently, more than ever, recent incidents occurred in the Malaysian work environment that challenged the traditional approach to a career path that provides steady career growth and lifetime employment in a single organisation (Ng et al., 2020). These challenges, in turn, may have a wide-ranging impact on individuals' career well-being. Bester et al. (2019) described career well-being as "individuals" long-term contentment with their career outcomes, career achievements, career changes and their sustainable employability amidst the complexities of the contemporary work environment. Employees' career well-being can be negatively affected due to closures of businesses, a large number of corporate job redundancies, recruitment and career advancement freezes and other unanticipated events that are taking place in the world of work due to COVID-19 (Sharudin, 2020).

Even though the traditional approach to career path development is still alive in Malaysia, recent evidence indicates that in a VUCA career environment, achieving objective career success within a single organisation is becoming less and less relevant and questionable (Lim, 2020). Hence why in the current chapter, we propose an approach to subjective career success that fulfils an individual's inner sense of purpose that leads to higher career well-being. There is some evidence suggesting that in an uncertain environment achieving subjective career success that fulfils intrinsic values is far more realistic when employees take the responsibility and personal agency for their career decisions (Lo Presti et al., 2018).

In order to remain employable in the post-COVID-19, VUCA career environment, employees should carefully self-manage their future career narrative, being flexible and adaptable to rapid changes. As suggested by contemporary career approaches, organisations have been less responsible for employee career management (Wiernik & Kostal, 2019). Add to this, with COVID-19, working from home is becoming a new norm. Though it brings a myriad of benefits for employees and employers, one simple question to ask is whether it may further impact the psychological contract between employees and the organisation leaving employees solely responsible for their own career self-management. Past findings have already alerted that within contemporary career approaches, conventional ideas of the psychological contracts in which organisations offer lifetime careers, job security and steady career advancement for employees' commitment and loyalty towards organisations have changed (Tietze & Nadin, 2011). According to protean and boundaryless approaches, objective career advancement is to those who effectively self-manage their careers by taking ownership of their own careers. Interestingly, Tietze and Nadin (2011) revealed that particularly women participants who worked from home in their study had indicated withdrawn behaviour from work both physically and emotionally, leaving the work 'where it should be' in relation to rest of life domains. They also have reported better work-life balance and work performance. Their findings support the notion that protean career-oriented women are better able to integrate both work and family responsibilities and achieve subjective career success compared to women who rely on traditional career paths. This will provide an interesting angle to explore as to how the new work environment may provide opportunities for the Malaysian workforce to take a personal agency in their own career decisions and re-define their career success.

9.2.3 Career self-management

Findings of the last two decades of research on contemporary careers suggest that employees who embrace value-driven, self-directed boundaryless career attitudes and behaviours adapt well to changing demands in the work environment and they report higher levels of career success and career-related well-being (Gunasekara et al., 2021; Hall et al., 2018; Lo Presti et al., 2018). Individual's career success does not occur in a vacuum. Among the myriad of personal, organisational and environmental factors that influence one's career success, career adaptability is one main factor that influences it (Uy et al., 2015). Career adaptability is generally considered as a meta competency that enables the career actor to develop other personal competencies, including openness to change and handle stresses in the new environment. So that the person can integrate well into the contemporary career landscape. In an era that organisations are increasingly trying to pass career management responsibilities to employees, researchers emphasise the significance of mastering career self-management skills (Hirschi, 2012). Researchers further argue that self-awareness and self-regulation are essential characteristics that drive the career self-management process (Hall et al., 2018). For instance, past findings suggest that a high level of self-awareness promotes clarity in self-identity, motivating employees to explore their authentic personal values, interests and career-related goals.

Moreover, Hirschi (2012) proposed a framework with four categories that can be used in career self-management. In that, the researcher suggested: (1) human capital resources (e.g., knowing how – knowledge, skills, attitudes and other characteristics) as necessary to achieve performance demands, (2) social capitals (e.g., knowing whom – social relations, network and their power of influence), (3) psychological resource (e.g., knowing why – career resilience, psychological mobility) and (4) identity resources (e.g., self-identity clarity, career goal clarity) as critical career-related resource essential for career self-development in a current career context.

9.2.4 Outcomes of contemporary career behaviour

Literature concerning careers of entrepreneurs proposes that protean and boundaryless career mindsets (specifically proactive career behaviour and preference towards physical and psychological mobility) as contributing factors for entrepreneurial intention (Baluku et al., 2018). Authors further argue that participants with proactive career behaviours and attitudes are more likely to choose the entrepreneurial path as it may provide more opportunities for career development in the VUCA environment. Similarly, Uy et al. (2015) found that entrepreneurial alertness as a trait to be mediated between proactive personality, boundaryless career mindset and career adaptability. In a similar vein, we can argue that the current environment may provide opportunities for individuals with the boundaryless and protean career attitude to explore completely new and value fulfilling career opportunities that go beyond the traditional career development path.

It is also worth mentioning that not only career actors who benefit from contemporary career approaches. Referring to the concept of 'protean paradox' (i.e., employees with protean career attitude may also become better corporate citizens, despite the belief that self-directed value-driven employees may be more self-focused, not organisationally focused), research also suggests that organisations benefit by employing people with protean and boundaryless career behaviours (Hall et al., 2018). Because those employees with proactive career behaviours develop new networks, acquire new competencies, and are intrinsically motivated to achieve psychological success, they are more likely to perform better at work. In contrast, Supeli and Creed's (2016) study found that in their Indonesian sample, employees with protean orientation are less committed to their organisation, less satisfied with their job, and the turnover intention is higher. The authors explained the reason for these contradictory findings as cultural and organisational values promoted in Asian organisations that do not support employees to grow based on their core values. Although this was a study on Indonesian employees, both Malaysians and Indonesians shared many common beliefs and values about life (Jaafar et al., 2012). Hence these findings might alert the organisations and employees in Malaysia about their level of readiness to follow contemporary career approaches in the current environment.

9.3 Method

In this study, desktop research adopting the scoping review approach was carried out. The purpose was to explore the body of the literature about career management, both in general and in Malaysia. Scoping review is suitable to be used when there is a broad amount of evidence pertaining to an emerging issue (Munn et al., 2018). It could provide a broad overview or mapping key concepts and evidence of a particular phenomenon (Whittemore et al., 2014), in this case, the post-COVID-19 career management phenomenon in Malaysia. These works could then be used for a systematic literature review at a later stage (Peterson, et al., 2017) or to synthesise future research (Arksey & O'Malley, 2005; Munn et al., 2018). Unlike systematic literature review, scoping review would select various kinds of literature related to a phenomenon. These literature include quantitative or qualitative journal articles, conference papers and any literature on the internet (Arksey & O'Malley, 2005). The process of conducting a scoping review involved the determination of search criteria of the literature, criteria for inclusion and exclusion, as well as collating and summarising the findings (Arksey & O'Malley, 2005). The findings could be presented in any way that could help the readers to understand the phenomenon.

9.3.1 Search strategy and search criteria

There were two categories of search. The first category was a search for journal articles pertaining to theories on career development as well as empirical studies in this topic. The second category was a search for current news pertaining to the impact of COVID-19 on the Malaysian business environment.

In the first category of search, the electronic search engines EBSCOHost (Academic Search Complete, Business Source Ultimate, Health Business Elite) Scopus, and Web of Science. The keywords for the search included "career success", "career protean career", "subjective values" and "career adaptability". These were the terms used in the literature on career success. We only select articles from 2018 onwards. This was to ensure the findings are close to the pandemic situation when the studies were carried out. Where needed, we did a cross-check to relevant previous studies prior to 2018 to obtain a comparison of findings, and we also included seminal articles published prior to 2018 on relevant career management constructs used in the chapter.

In the second category of search, we used Google search engine, news agencies such as *Bernama* (the Malaysian national news agency) or Reuters Malaysia, to search for news updates in Malaysia. The keywords for the search were "unemployment rate", "employment rate", "COVID-19", "career development", "career prospect", "business failure" and "economic". All news that occurred in Malaysia from 2019 to March 2021 were selected for analysis.

9.3.2 Criteria for inclusion and exclusion

For those articles selected in the first category of search, we only included those in the English language only and published in peer-reviewed academic journals. All conceptual and empirical articles, both quantitative and qualitative, were included. Our initial searches yielded a total of 21 journal articles. We refined our initial sample of articles by scanning titles, abstracts and keywords. We then further refined our selection by excluding conference proceedings.

For those news articles selected under the second category, we further refined by only including news from the official government sources or other reputable sources such as the Department of Statistics Malaysia. In addition, we only included news that reported actual statistics from reliable sources and commentaries from experts, such as investment analysts, etc. For experts' commentaries that cited some statistics, we further cross-checked the publication from official government sources, if available, to ensure reliability. We have excluded any commentaries from non-experts that could be speculative in nature.

9.3.3 Collating, summarising and reporting the findings

At this stage, the selected literature of each category was organised, using the Table function on MS Word, based on the themes (Arksey &

O'Malley, 2005). The themes, which were based on the objectives of this study, were unemployment, organisation support, career success and career management. A summary was written on each piece of literature, and these summaries were then combined and reported in the findings section below.

9.4 Findings

9.4.1 The impact of pandemic on unemployment and job insecurity

According to the Department of Statistics Malaysia, April 2020 reported the highest unemployment rate in 2020, being 5% or 778,800 individuals being unemployed. This was the second month since the Movement Control Order (MCO) was enforced on March 18 (Shah et al., 2020). The MCO not only restricted the movement of people but also locked down a vast majority of the economic sectors in the country. Only the essential industries could operate during that time. Many businesses were either closed down or downsized in the following few months. The unemployment rate in November stood at 4.8%, with 764,400 individuals being unemployed (Department of Statistics Malaysia, 2021). In fact, the unemployment rates were hovering between 4.5% and 4.8% since April 2020. With the third wave of COVID-19 infection since October 2020 (Rampal & Liew, 2021), the unemployment rate would need a much longer period to reverse back to its norm of 3% before the pandemic.

These phenomena highlighted the gloomy economic environment that all businesses in Malaysia need to sustain, at least in the medium term, before experiencing a full recovery. This could also suggest the possible decline in the current job market, especially in the major economic sectors. An online study conducted by Randstad Malaysia with 531 Malaysian working professionals in June and July 2020 to understand the pandemic sentiments of the workforce (Randstad, n.d.). The survey reported that 91% of the respondents intended upskilling or re-skilling within the next 12 months. Among these, 55% of them would do so in preparation for process automation and digitisation, 21% planned to change their career or industry that they are currently in, 13% quoted fear of losing jobs while 8% worried about the sustainability of their current employers' businesses. The outcomes of this survey suggested that employees need to take a proactive role in their career choices to achieve career success (Ling et al., 2017; Wiernik & Kostal, 2019). Moreover, having more career resources (Hirschi, 2012) are always essential to navigate through such times of uncertainty.

9.4.2 The expectation gap of employers and employees

9.4.2.1 The sources of career development

Up to December 2019, small and medium enterprises (SMEs) were contributing jobs in agriculture (41.4%), construction (48.3%), service (50.5%), manufacturing (46.7%), mining and quarrying (28.1%), giving an average total of 48.4% of the total workforce (Department of Statistics Malaysia, 2020). Being a major stakeholder in the economic entity of a nation, SMEs play a pivotal role in providing career paths for the employees in the country (Khai et al., 2020). Zakaria et al. (2020) observed that SMEs offer career development through job enrichment, allowing creativity in work and more involvement in the management process. However, with the significant adverse impact of the pandemic, the MCO and MCO 2.0 that took place in the 12 months' period (March 2020 to February 2021), many SMEs were not able to survive even in the short term due to limited working capital (Khai et al., 2020). Hence, company survival was the highest priority for SMEs. Expecting employers to provide career growth in such a challenging time might not be too desirable.

Despite all these setbacks, according to Nathan (2020), employees are expecting SMEs to give more support in their career development. This was based on a survey carried out in November 2020 on 500 SME employees by an international professional online HR agency. The survey reported that 58% of the respondents placed career growth as the top consideration when looking at job changes, with work-life balance at 49% and more rewards and recognition at 31%. These signify that most employees in Malaysia are still placing a high reliance on employers for career development. Such an expectation could be carried forward from the prepandemic time. However, this expectation would require recalibration with the change in the post-pandemic economic climate that affected most businesses adversely.

The reliance of the employees on employers for career development and career success is not new. Kiong and Yin-Fah (2016) took a survey of 352 academic staff in Malaysian private universities and reported that employees' perceived employability was the strongest predictor of career success. It was also found that individual protean career attitude and organisational learning practices are correlated with perceived employability and career success. Organisational learning practices were the strongest contribution towards career success (Kiong & Yin-Fah, 2016). Organisational learning practices include the provision of staff training and development that enhanced their employability. This study involved academic staff where training and development are utmost important in their current job and career. However, employers in the SMEs might perceive organisational learning practices as optional, placing it at a lower priority for funding (Neckebrouck et al., 2018), especially in the challenging post-pandemic time.

9.4.2.2 Flexible work arrangement

The survey by Nathan (2020) reported that 52% of the respondents expect more flexible work arrangement support to be provided by the employers. Flexible work arrangements include work-from-home, flexible working hours, shift work, fraction work as well as part-time work (Gainey & Clenney, 2006; Hornung et al., 2008; Ramakrishnan & Arokiasamy, 2019; Secret, 2000). Employees can better manage their responsibilities under flexible work arrangements. These arrangements could also help the employees to achieve work-life balance (Chung & Van der Lippe, 2018). From the employers' perspective, these arrangements could help improve employee productivity and organisational profitability (Ramakrishnan & Arokiasamy, 2019). However, even though large organisations could implement flexible work arrangements more efficiently with more resources at their disposal, most SMEs in Malaysia have little flexibility in their work arrangement. This limitation was mainly due to the lack of good information technology infrastructure and digitisation within the companies to support flexible work arrangements (Khai et al., 2020; Yi, 2020). Indeed, such infrastructure demands a considerable amount of capital investment which is above the funding capability of most SMEs. Moreover, although the culture of flexible work arrangement has been encouraged by many stakeholders, it is still not widely practised (Ahmad et al., 2016).

9.4.3 The conceptual framework

Figure 9.1 depicts a conceptual framework of the contemporary career environment, the impact on individual career self-management and the role of organisational support in supporting employees' career self-management. Drawing on the discussion, the proposed framework provides insights to issues faced by employees in Malaysia in the current COVID-19 context and how contemporary career approaches can be potential solutions to manage those challenges. It also highlighted the essential initiatives that both individuals and organisations could take to reap the benefits for both parties.

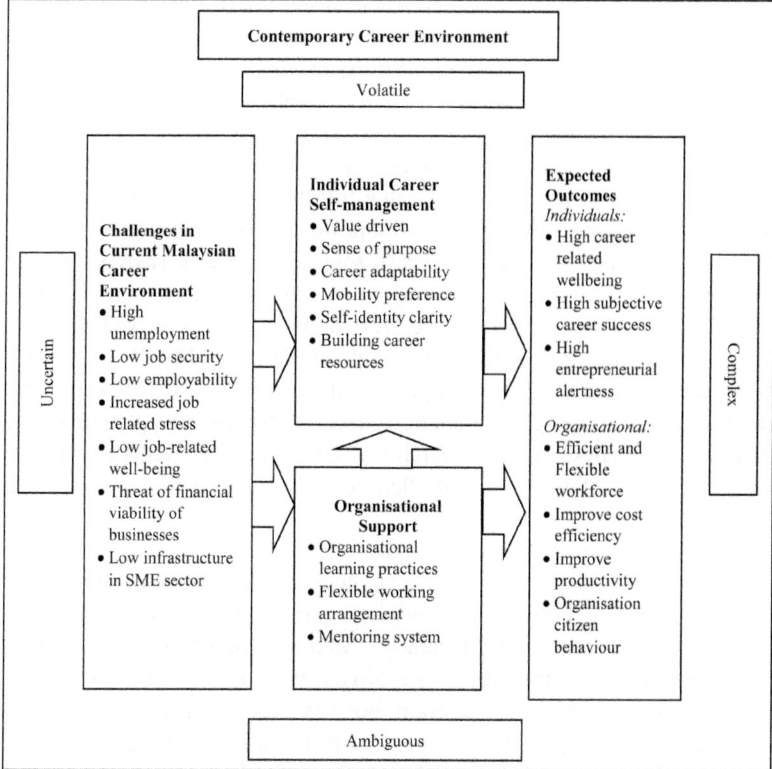

Figure 9.1 Conceptual framework of contemporary career environment, its impact on individual career self-management, and the role of organisations in supporting employees' careers self-management

9.5 Conclusion

9.5.1 Theoretical implications

Our findings show that employees in Malaysia rely on employers for their career development and achieving career success. However, these organisational dependent mindsets are now being challenged with the economic downturn resulting from the pandemic. Short-term survival and business transformation, especially those that have been pushed to move towards digital platforms, are the utmost priorities of many businesses. Hence, employers are no longer reliable suppliers of initiatives that could help the employees to grow and achieve their career goals. Employees need to develop a mindset of a contemporary career to improving their employability, career success and sense of meaning in life.

The findings have important practical implications on employees as well as on researchers, HR practitioners and career counsellors. For the employees, they need to take control of their career choices and decisions so that they can craft more value fulfilling careers. However, there is a lack of awareness of such a need among the working class in society. Employee unions could play an active role in promoting such a mindset through seminars and forums. Currently, government agencies such as the Ministry of Human Resource Development are conducting upskilling and re-skilling programmes through PENJANA HRDF to help the affected employees seeking new opportunities (Sunil, 2020). However, the training programmes could include courses on transferable generic skills, such as data analysis skills, research skills and creativity skills that could meet the needs of Industry 4.0 (Benešová & Tupa, 2017) and enhance employability.

From the employers' perspective, these findings highlighted some of the work arrangements that could benefit them. These include flexible working hours, fraction hours, work from home or job sharing. These arrangements could improve cost efficiency as well as productivity. The human resource practices, especially those SMEs, would need to be revisited, reviewed, or re-arranged. Relevant policies and procedures pertaining to these work arrangements would need to be established. Such arrangements might require employers to invest in technology infrastructure and digitisation of some operational processes. The initial painstaking process would be inevitable, but in the long-term, these investments will be justified in terms of operational efficiency and, perhaps, better the quality of services provided.

From the theoretical point of view, these findings should stimulate discussions and research on how employees shift their mindsets from traditional organisational career orientation to protean career and career adaptability to meet the current environmental challenges. In addition, more empirical research is needed to test the existing theories that were valid in the pre-pandemic era. With the drastic change in the social and business environment, the existing theories might need revision or even new theories are needed to provide an insight on how employees shift their paradigm on their control over their career decisions to enjoy better value fulfilling careers. In conclusion, in an uncertain environment, employees need to take responsibility and personal agency for their career decisions to achieve subjective career success that fulfils intrinsic values.

9.5.2 Practical implications

This chapter contributes to the knowledge of career management in the Malaysian context. Employees could benefit from the findings of the literature review. They could reflect on their own beliefs on career management and make the needed adjustments to adapt to the post-COVID-19 career environment. These adjustments might include psychological as well as career resources. In a turbulent time, these adjustments could be seen as a life jacket, providing a safety measure for the passenger.

This chapter also contributes to the knowledge of the human resource policy formulation of Malaysian employers. Despite financial challenges and the threat of sustainability, employers could still provide the needed support to the employees to self-manage their careers. These supports could be some human resource policies and practices that could benefit the employers as well when implemented effectively. With more deliberation and dissemination, these policies and practices could lead to more conversations among employers to create a conducive environment for employees to self-manage their careers.

9.5.3 Future research directions

A change in the employment landscape in Malaysia due to the pandemic encourages both the employees and the employers to re-think about the concept of career and how it affects employee's sense of career fulfilment. Based on the contemporary career constructs mentioned in this chapter, we propose a research agenda that may be worth exploring for the benefit of both employees and human resource practitioners.

9.5.3.1 Use of human capital resources to enhance employability and value fulfilling career

Morrison and Hall (2002) highlighted the need for an employee to develop multiple competencies. Such competencies are essential as the landscape of employment is very volatile. Employees need to have a paradigm shift to adapt to this change. Research is needed to find out how employees perceive their knowledge, skills and abilities (KSA) as securities of their jobs and how they intend to acquire more KSA to become a tool to hedge the risk of unemployment. In addition, it will be beneficial to know what hinders them from exploring new KSA and their perception about human capital resources as part of their career resources for a more fulfilling career in the Malaysian context. The country' culture could be an active agent in shaping the employees' mindset on career decisions. A research on culture and career decisions might shed some light on this enchanted area.

For the employers, organisational learning practices were found to be a major contributor of employees' perceived career success (Kiong & Yin-Fah, 2016). Organisational learning practices encompass diverse types of training and development. HR managers should ensure the employees are equipped with generic skills which could be transferable between jobs. These skills are essential for employability. In a VUCA environment, it is critical for organisations to have a flexible workforce which could allow changes to be made with ease in the needed tasks and team structure. This could also help improve business sustainability. Research could examine the effectiveness of different types of generic skill training and the transferability of these skills after the training. The outcome of this research could help the HR practitioners to determine suitable training methods for optimum results.

9.5.3.2 Use of social capital resources to enhance employability and value fulfilling careers

The Malaysian society is closely knitted, with a culture of high collectivism (Noordin & Jusoff, 2010). They make decisions collectively, and older people usually have high respect from the younger generations. Hence, older people could be role models and provide helpful advice to the young in the capacity of a mentor (Abiddin, 2012). Hence, it might be worth exploring the impact of having a career mentor.

9.5.3.3 Use of psychological and career identity resources to achieve career success

Psychological resources refer to positive psychological traits and states that are related to the work role (Hirschi, 2012). These include open-mindedness, optimism, self-efficacy beliefs and proactive personality. Career identity resources, on the other hand, are the conscious awareness of how one views oneself in relation to one's work. These two resources could affect job burnout and career turnover intentions (Barthauer et al., 2020). Future research could explore how these psychological resources are being developed and how they could affect career success.

Summary

- Due to the COVID-19 pandemic, the rate of unemployment in Malaysia is record high, and the survival of SMEs is alarming.
- Employees still rely on traditional organisational career orientation.

- Malaysian workforce needs to develop a contemporary career attitude to improve their employability, career success and sense of meaning in life.
- In the midst of a myriad of challenges faced by organisations, they should support employees to self-manage their careers by implementing effective learning practices, flexible work arrangements and mentoring systems.
- In an uncertain environment achieving subjective career success that fulfils intrinsic values is far more realistic when employees take responsibility and personal agency in their career decisions.

References

Abiddin, N. Z. (2012). The sources to acquire informal mentor on the graduate agricultural entrepreneurs in Malaysia. *International Journal of Engineering Education*, *1*(1), 209–217.

Ahmad, A., Shaw, N. E., Bown, N. J., Gardiner, J., & Omar, K. (2016). The impact of negative work home interface on intention to leave and the role of flexible working arrangements in Malaysia. *The Journal of Developing Areas*, *50*(5), 507–515. Retrieved from https://www.jstor.org/stable/26415615

Arksey, H., & O'Malley, L. (2005). Scoping studies: towards a methodological framework. *International Journal of Social Research Methodology*, *8*(1), 19–32. https://doi.org/10.1080/1364557032000119616

Baluku, M. M., Löser, D., Otto, K., & Schummer, S. E. (2018). Career mobility in young professionals: How a protean career personality and attitude shapes international mobility and entrepreneurial intentions. *Journal of Global Mobility*, *6* (1), 102–122. https://doi.org/10.1108/JGM-10-2017-0041

Barthauer, L., Kaucher, P., Spurk, D., & Kauffeld, S. (2020). Burnout and career (un) sustainability: Looking into the Blackbox of burnout triggered career turnover intentions. *Journal of Vocational Behavior*, *117*, 103334. https://doi.org/10.1016/j.jvb.2019.103334

Benešová, A., & Tupa, J. (2017). Requirements for education and qualification of people in Industry 4.0. *Procedia Manufacturing*, *11*, 2195–2202. https://doi.org/10.1016/j.promfg.2017.07.366

Bester, M., Coetzee, M., Ferreira, N., & Potgieter, I. L. (2019). *Conceptualisation of Future-Fit Career Wellbeing. Personal Conversation among Authors.* University of South Africa Pretoria, South Africa.

Bravo, J., Seibert, S. E., Kraimer, M. L., Wayne, S. J., & Liden, R. C. (2017). Measuring career orientations in the era of the boundaryless career. *Journal of Career Assessment*, *25*, 502–525. https://doi.org/10.1177%2F1069072715616107

Briscoe, J., & Hall, D. (2006). The interplay of boundaryless and protean careers: Combinations and implications. *Journal of Vocational Behavior*, *69*(1), 4–18. https://doi.org/10.1016/j.jvb.2005.09.002

Chung, H., & Van der Lippe, T. (2018). Flexible working, work–life balance, and gender equality: Introduction. *Social Indicators Research*, 1–17. https://doi.org/10.1007/s11205-018-2025-x

Department of Statistics Malaysia. (2020, July 29). *Small and Medium Enterprises (SMEs) Performance 2019.* https://www.dosm.gov.my

Department of Statistics Malaysia. (2020, June 15). *Key Statistics of Labour Force in Malaysia, April 2020.* https://www.dosm.gov.my

Department of Statistics Malaysia. (2021, January 11). *Key Statistics of Labour Force in Malaysia, November 2020.* https://www.dosm.gov.my

Gainey, T. W., & Clenney, B. F. (2006). Flextime and telecommuting: Examining individual perceptions. *Southern Business Review*, *32*(1), 13–21. Retrieved from https://www.journalguide.com/journals/southern-business-review

Gunasekara, A., Bertone, S., Almeida, S., & Crowley-Henry, M. (2021). Dancing to two tunes: The role of bicultural identity and strong ties in skilled migrants' value-driven protean careers. *International Journal of Intercultural Relations, 81*, 42–53. https://doi.org/10.1016/j.ijintrel.2020.12.007

Hall, D. T., Yip, J., & Doiron, K. (2018). Protean careers at work: self-direction and values orientation in psychological success. *Annual Review of Organizational Psychology and Organizational Behavior*, *5*, 129–156. https://doi.org/10.1146/annurev-orgpsych-032117-104631

Hirschi, A. (2012). The career resources model: an integrative framework for career counsellors, *British Journal of Guidance & Counselling*, *40*(4), 369–383, https://doi.org/10.1080/03069885.2012.700506

Hirschi, A., Jaensch, V. K., & Herrmann, A. (2017). Protean career orientation, vocational identity, and self-efficacy: an empirical clarification of their relationship. *European Journal of Work and Organizational Psychology*, *26*(2), 208–220.

Hornung, S., Rousseau, D. M., & Glaser, J. (2008). Creating flexible work arrangements through idiosyncratic deals. *Journal of applied psychology*, *93*(3), 655–664. https://doi.org/10.1037/00219010.93.3.655

Jaafar, J. L., Idris, M. A., Ismuni, J., Fei, Y., Jaafar, S., Ahmad, Z., & Sugandi, Y. S. (2012). The sources of happiness to the Malaysians and Indonesians: data from a smaller nation. *Procedia-Social and Behavioral Sciences*, *65*, 549–556. https://doi.org/10.1016/j.sbspro.2012.11.164

Khai, K. G., Onn, Y. W., Zulkifli, R. B., Kandasamy, S., & Ahmad, A. B. (2020). The necessity to digitize SMEs Business Model during the COVID-19 Pandemic period to remain sustainable in Malaysia. *Journal of Education and Social Sciences*, *16*(1), 73–81. Retrieved from https://www.jesoc.com/wp-content/uploads/2020/12/JESOC16-032.pdf

Kiong, T. P., & Yin-Fah, B. C. (2016). Exploring factors towards career success in Malaysia. *International Business Management*, *10*(17), 3936–3943. https://doi.org/10.36478/ibm.2016.3936.3943

Kuriakose, S & Tran, T. (2020). *Impacts of COVID-19 on Firms in Malaysia: Results from the 1st Round of COVID-19 Business Pulse Survey.* World Bank, Washington, DC. © World Bank. https://openknowledge.worldbank.org/handle/10986/34965

Lim, I. (2020, August 13). *For Malaysian employees, flexi hours, work-life balance top reasons for happiness; salary levels leading cause of dissatisfaction*. The Malay Mail. https://www.malaymail.com/news/malaysia/2020/08/13/for-malaysian-employees-flexi-hours-work-life-balance-top-reasons-for-happi/1893469

Ling, N. P., Bandar, N. F. A., Halim, F. A., & Muda, A. L. (2017). Proactive behaviour as a mediator in the relationship between quality of work life and career success. *International Journal of Business and Society, 18*(S4), 701–709. http://www.ijbs.unimas.my/images/repository/pdf/Vol18-s4-paper7.pdf

Lo Presti, A., Pluviano, S., & Briscoe, J.P. (2018). Are freelancers a breed apart? The role of protean and boundaryless career attitudes in employability and career success. *Human Resource Management Journal, 28*, 427–442. https://doi.org/10.1111/1748-8583.12188

Morrison, R.F., & Hall, D.T. (2002). Career adaptability. In D.T. Hall (Ed.), *Careers In and Out of Organizations* (pp. 205–233). Thousand Oaks, CA: Sage.

Munn, Z., Peters, M. D., Stern, C., Tufanaru, C., McArthur, A., & Aromataris, E. (2018). Systematic review or scoping review? Guidance for authors when choosing between a systematic or scoping review approach. *BMC Medical Research Methodology, 18*(1), 1–7. https://doi.org/10.1186/s12874-018-0611-x

Nathan. (2020, December 4). SME employees expect support for career growth. *The Malaysian* https://themalaysianreserve.com/2020/12/04/sme-employees-expect-support-for-career-growth/

Neckebrouck, J., Schulze, W., & Zellweger, T. (2018). Are family firms good employers? *Academy of Management Journal, 61*(2), 553–585. https://doi.org/10.5465/amj.2016.0765

Ng, S. I., Lim, Q. H., Cheah, J. H., Ho, J. A., & Tee, K. K. (2020). A moderated-mediation model of career adaptability and life satisfaction among working adults in Malaysia. *Current Psychology*, 1–15. https://doi.org/10.1007/s12144-020-00837-7

Nishanthi, M.N., & Kailasapathay, P. (2017). Employee commitment: The role of organisational socialization and protean career orientation. *South Asian Journal of Human Resource Management, 5*(1), 1–27.

Noordin, F., & Jusoff, K. (2010). Individualism-collectivism and job satisfaction between Malaysia and Australia. *International Journal of Educational Management, 24*(2), 159–174. https://doi.org/10.1108/09513541011020963

Peterson, J., Pearce, P. F., Ferguson, L. A., & Langford, C. A. (2017). Understanding scoping reviews: Definition, purpose, and process. *Journal of the American Association of Nurse Practitioners, 29*(1), 12–16. https://doi.org/10.1002/2327-6924.12380

Ramakrishnan, S., & Arokiasamy, L. (2019). Flexible working arrangements in Malaysia: a study of employee's performance on white collar employees. *Global Business and Management Research, 11*(1), 551–559. https://search.proquest.com/scholarly-journals/flexible-working-arrangements-malaysia-study/docview/2236125482/se-2?accountid=14205

Rampal, L., & Liew, B. S. (2021). Malaysia's third COVID-19 wave - a paradigm shift required. *The Medical Journal of Malaysia, 76*(1), 1–4. http://www.e-mjm.org/2021/v76n1/third-COVID-19-wave.pdf

Randstad. (n.d.). *91% of respondents are motivated to upskill and re-skill in the next 12 months.* https://www.randstad.com.my/workforce-insights/talent-management/91-per-cent-are-motivated-to-upskill-and-re-skill/

Secret, M. (2000). Identifying the family, job, and workplace characteristics of employees who use work-family benefits. *Family Relations, 49*(2), 217–225. https://doi.org/10.1111/j.1741-3729.2000.00217.x

Shah, A. U. M., Safri, S. N. A., Thevadas, R., Noordin, N. K., Abd Rahman, A., Sekawi, Z., & Sultan, M. T. H. (2020). COVID-19 outbreak in Malaysia: Actions taken by the Malaysian government. *International Journal of Infectious Diseases, 97*, 108–116. https://doi.org/10.1016/j.ijid.2020.05.093

Sharudin, A.H. (2020, October 22). *A quarter of Malaysian workers fear job loss—survey.* The Edge Markets. https://www.theedgemarkets.com/article/quarter-malaysian-workers-fear-job-loss-%E2%80%94-survey

Sullivan, S.E., & Arthur, M.B. (2006). The evolution of the boundaryless career concept: Examining physical and psychological mobility. *Journal of Vocational Behavior, 69*, 19–29. https://doi.org/10.1016/j.jvb.2005.09.001

Sunil, P. (2020, June 24). More than 20,000 job opportunities to be offered through PENJANA HRDF. *Human Resources Online.* https://www.humanresourcesonline.net/more-than-20-000-job-opportunities-to-be-offered-through-penjana-hrdf

Surendran, S. (2020, June 20). The State of the Nation: An opportune time to reinvent Malaysia's labour market. *The Edge Weekly.* https://www.theedgemarkets.com/article/state-nation-opportune-time-reinvent-malaysias-labour-market

Supeli, A., & Creed, P. A. (2016). The longitudinal relationship between protean career orientation and job satisfaction, organizational commitment, and intention-to-quit. *Journal of Career Development, 43*(1), 66–80. https://doi.org/10.1177%2F0894845315581686

Tietze, S., & Nadin, S. (2011). The psychological contract and the transition from office-based to home-based work: Homeworking and the psychological contract. *Human Resource Management Journal, 21*(3), 318–334. https://doi.org/10.1111/j.1748-8583.2010.00137.x

Uy, M.A., Chan, K., Sam, Y.L., Ho, M.R., & Chernyshenko, O.S. (2015). Proactivity, adaptability and boundaryless career attitudes: The mediating role of entrepreneurial alertness. *Journal of Vocational Behavior, 86*, 115–123. https://doi.org/10.1016/j.jvb.2014.11.005

Whittemore, R., Chao, A., Jang, M., Minges, K. E., & Park, C. (2014). Methods for knowledge synthesis: an overview. *Heart & Lung, 43*(5), 453–461. https://doi.org/10.1016/j.hrtlng.2014.05.014

Wiernik, B. M., & Kostal, J. W. (2019). Protean and boundaryless career orientations: A critical review and meta-analysis. *Journal of Counseling Psychology, 66*(3), 280-307. https://doi.org/10.1037/cou0000324

Yi, V. Z. (2020). *Struggle of Malaysian SMEs during the COVID-19 Pandemic. Findings from Webinar: SMEs beyond the MCO – Lessons from the PRIHATIN Stimulus.* KSI Strategic Institute for Asia Pacific. https://kasi.asia/wp-content/

uploads/2020/05/KSI-Policy-Brief-Struggle-of-Malaysian-SMEs-During-the-COVID-19-Pandemic.pdf

Zakaria, N. S., Yussof, K. Y. S. K. M., Ibrahim, D., & Tibok, R. P. (2020). Career after graduation: Future graduates' perceptions of job attributes in small and medium enterprises (SMEs) and multi-national corporations (MNCs). *Journal of Social Sciences and Humanities*, *17*(6), 252–264. https://ejournal.ukm.my/ebangi/article/view/41260